THE
SAINTS AND MARTYRS
OF IRELAND

THE
SAINTS AND MARTYRS
OF IRELAND

H. Patrick Montague

COLIN SMYTHE
Gerrards Cross 1981

Copyright © 1981 H. Patrick Montague

First published in 1981 by Colin Smythe Limited,
Gerrards Cross, Buckinghamshire

British Library Cataloguing in Publication Data

Montague, H. Patrick
    The saints and martyrs of Ireland.
    1. Saints – Ireland
    I. Title
    274.15   BR1710
    ISBN 0-86140-106-9
    ISBN 0-86140,107-7 Pbk

Printed in Great Britain
Typesetting by Grove Graphics, Tring
Printed and bound by Billing & Sons Ltd.
Guildford, London, Worcester and Oxford

Contents

Preface

Books have a habit of reflecting a personal interest over many years on the part of the author. Similarly, the choice of material and the emphasis placed on one aspect or another of the final production is often the result of personal convictions or experiences. This book is not only an example of this, but in some respects, arises directly from experiences which have lived in my memory as essential parts of that unwritten autobiography which is in all of us.

In early summer of 1944, I arrived in Taranto, Italy, as a Staff Officer of the Eighth Army. The next morning, I was urgently summoned to assist an American soldier who had driven his Jeep into the path of a procession of Italians who were celebrating the Feast of their local saint. Since nobody was hurt, the situation was quickly adjusted. I was able to deal with it in Italian, aided by the presence of a local priest. Between us we calmed the excited people and rescued the soldier from his awkward predicament.

In conversation later, the priest informed me that the Saint was Cataldo, and it was common knowledge over the whole of Southern Italy that he was Irish. I wondered at the time whether this unusual fact was so well-known in Ireland. In the years which followed, I have often pondered on the strange anomaly that the memory of Irish exiles like Cathal, or Cataldo, of Taranto, can inspire public holidays and gatherings of the faithful all over Europe, and receive no more than a brief reference in works of scholarship in Ireland.

About a year after this incident, I had occasion to stop for a short time in a small Italian town not far from Venice. The name of the town was San Dona del Piave. I had already heard of the Irish saint, Donato of Fiesole, and enquired if this Church and town were dedicated to him. A short talk with the priest brought the information that the Patron was indeed San Donato, the medieval Bishop of Fiesole, the subject throughout the North of Italy of a cult comparable to that of San Cataldo in the South.

I served from 1945 till the end of 1948 in Trieste. So, to add

7

to the quite fortuitous experiences described above, I found that one of the more interesting people living there was the late Stanislaus Joyce who had lived there for many years with his famous brother, James, the celebrated modern Irish writer. Apart from interesting comments on his collaboration with his brother, Stanislaus was well-informed on the history of Irish saints in the north of Italy and in Austria. He also brought me into contact with several Italian scholars who had made a special study of Irish saints.

It is not, perhaps, surprising that I developed a special interest in the veneration of Irish people created, developed, and sustained by those who are not Irish. This, I believe, is a fact of Irish history of which the Irish should be aware, perhaps more than they are. It cannot be without significance that so many foreigners survey our country through an ancient devotion to our representatives. Nor can it be without significance that all of our canonised saints were raised to the honours of the altar, mainly by the efforts and devout support of faithful outside Ireland. Even the most recent of these, Oliver Plunkett, moved into the last stages of his canonisation when his intercession brought a miraculous cure in an Italian hospital. It is timely to recall that Ireland entered into this final process, principally because it was an Irish nun in the hospital who invoked his aid for a patient. St. Patrick himself has been the continued object of veneration in the Touraine in France, since before he started his mission in Ireland.

It is, in effect, the universal image of our people which lies deep in the thinking which led to this book. Every chapter has been chosen with this in mind. So it seemed relevant to describe our canonised Saints, but equally relevant to enquire into the attitude of the Church to all Irish saints, as creations of popular veneration. Equally, within the universal context, it was worth a comment that some Irish martyrs have recently been awarded official status by the Holy See, although they were part of an English List.

This is an extremely short volume which touches on a wide topic, or indeed a series of topics. The most an author can do is to specify the limits within which he is working, and then indicate the main sources of interest. Having done that, he would hope that his readers would avail themselves of the vast body of literature which deals in detail with whatever attracts their attention.

Acknowledgements

I wish to thank oll those who assisted me in the preparation of this volume: the *Catholic Herald*; *Ireland's Own*; the Irish-American Institute, publishers of Mary Ryan D'Arcy's *The Saints of Ireland*; Fr. Bernard J. Canning, author of *Irish Born Secular Priests of Scotland*. All have kindly allowed me to use material from their publications. I was also granted permission by Mme. and M. Lerou of the Comité Nationale St. Fiacre to quote from material published by the Comité, and they also very kindly gave me valuable information that they themselves had gathered as part of their doctoral dissertation at the Sorbonne on St. Fiacre of Meaux.

I am indebted to the Oxford University Press for permission to quote information on St. Egbert from *The Oxford Dictionary of Saints*, and to John Donald Ltd., of Edinburgh for permission to quote the entry on the Schottenklöster in Gordon Donaldson and Robert Morpeth's *Dictionary of Scottish History*.

I am most grateful to the following for their helpful advice: His Eminence Cardinal Tomas O'Fiach, Primate of All Ireland, himself a distinguished Irish historian, kindly drew my attention to the Committee of Ecclesiastical Historians who are currently revising the list of Irish Martyrs. As a result, many helpful comments came from Fr. Benignus Millett, OFM, and it was from this source that correspondence between me and the Procurator of Franciscan Causes, Fr. Mario Cairoli, OFM, led to a stimulating and informative meeting in Rome. In addition, Mgr. Mario Oliveri, of the Apostolic Delegation in London, has given constant guidance on important points in the text.

Finally, authorities outside Ireland have been of great assistance. The Archdiocese of Lucca, Italy, has provided information on St. Fridian and St. Siollan; the Archdiocese of Chambery, France, in connexion with St. Concord, and the Diocese of Trier, Germany, in respect of St. Wendel. To all these and others, my thanks.   H.P.M.

Author's Note

As far as the evidence allows, relevant dates are recorded in the heading of each biographical note. On the left is the Feast-day. On the right is the date of birth, if known, followed by the date of death.

CHAPTER I

Introduction

"This day thou shalt be with me in Paradise". With these momentous words the Saviour Himself created the first Saint in the Christian Church. He also laid down the true definition of a Saint who is simply one who has attained, after death, the whole purpose of life, which is to enter into Heaven. The Good Thief is listed in the Roman Martyrology and in others which follow it as their basic authority. St. Dismas, the Good Thief, is the Patron of prisoners and of prisoners' reform and rehabilitation organisations, and not only in the Catholic Church.

The veneration of holy people is based on the conviction that they are in Heaven, and that their intercession can be invoked for that reason. Veneration of the dead is as old as human nature and is in no way the monopoly of any church. Even canonisation is not unique to the Church of Rome, nor does the Church of Rome exclude the fact that Heaven is populated by many non-Catholics. It is, in this connection, a fact of some significance that the oldest Saint listed in the Roman Martyrology is St. Abraham, the father of the Jewish people.

In the Catholic tradition, veneration of holy people was a local phenomenon from the beginnings of the Christian Faith. Like so many other traditions, it gradually grew into an institution when Bishops began, in their own Sees, to recognise the sanctity of one holy person after another, and to permit the faithful to practise their veneration publicly. In due course, the Holy See made the practice of canonisation more official still when, in 993 Pope John XV canonised St. Udalricus. Three more centuries were to pass during which the Holy See and Bishops of the Church were all participating in the same practice. Throughout all this, the faithful steadily maintained their traditional veneration, with or without the official recognition of either their Bishops or the Holy See.

Canonisation does not mean that traditional, spontaneous veneration has ceased, nor indeed that it is no longer allowed. There are many instances throughout the world where the

11

faithful turn for inspiration to a departed servant of God, and at any given time there is a long list of names which have been submitted to the Holy See for investigation for ultimate canonisation.

Allied to this whole process is the question of martyrdom. A martyr, in the widest sense, is one who accepts suffering and even death in pursuance of a principle. It is from the Saviour Himself that the highest ideal of martyrdom is handed on. In that ideal, the choice exists of abandoning the principle at issue, in exchange for an end to the suffering or in exchange for life itself. During the Reformation, it involved explicitly abandoning the Catholic Faith to put an end to persecution in all its forms.

In Ireland, as in England, during the Reformation and under the Penal Laws, every Catholic had what seemed a simple choice, to adhere to his or her Faith with all the penalties inherent in that choice, or to abandon it and obtain the freedom and security which followed. Their rejection of the second alternative during that period seems to have put great numbers of Catholics in both countries into the category of martyrs. For in addition to those who gave their lives, there were those who suffered imprisonment, transportation, torture and material deprivation.

The purpose of this study is to examine in as much detail as possible the Irish people who are regarded as saints. Such a study should cover all those cases which have been accepted as suitable for investigation and, of course, those who have ultimately been canonised. It is relevant also to refer to outstanding instances of widely practised veneration, even though these may not have become official Causes. There is clear evidence that the Holy See has given official sanction in many such cases, and has implicitly recognised others. It is important to stress the enormous prestige which a Papal investigation carries in the world of scholarship. Few institutions can compare with the Holy See in the field of historical research. Its resources in terms of research material and records are immense. The margin of error in the decisions of its Commissions of Enquiry is minimal, and indeed their conclusions can be regarded as final.

The people of Ireland have probably more reason than any other to appreciate the completeness and finality of Papal investigations. The outcome of these has special importance also in relation to canonisations. Irish leaders were often important figures in the Church, and like so many other leaders in history, their image sometimes has been distorted by the circumstances in which they lived. This was true of three of the canonised Saints of Ireland, particularly of Oliver Plunkett and to a lesser extent of

Laurence O'Toole and Virgilius of Salzburg. Canonisation, in these cases, has proved to be an adjustment of the historical record. Given the depth and authority of the investigations, it can safely be said that no historical doubts remain about the sanctity of any of them. Elevation to the honours of the altar is their vindication before the bar of history.

In this book, the careers of specific Saints and Scholars will be highlighted. This has been done many times before, but seldom has it been done with the purpose of demonstrating an eternal rather than an historical impact. Too often in the modern age, the Irishmen of the Golden Age are presented as models of sanctity who had nothing practical to offer and certainly nothing that is relevant to the present day. The lives and achievements of the Irish Saints and Scholars are not only a part of Irish history, but for centuries have pointed the way along which society should proceed at all times. In the widest sense, it is clear that the first manifestation of an Irish national image was the Golden Age. The missionaries and scholars were the first Irishmen to step out of the historic framework of the fragmented regionalism of Ireland, and to present the world outside with its first experience of a national Irish image. The fact that this was linked with the Universal Church of their day should be a valuable corrective to the contrary influences of modern society.

The credibility of investigations is of the utmost importance to the Church, and this is specially true of a canonisation. There must be no lingering doubt, just as there must be no lingering doubt about a dogma once it is proclaimed. It has been from the beginning of Christianity the practice of the Church to make traditions of long standing into institutions and that is the simple story behind most of its final pronouncements. Vox populi, vox Dei – the voice of the people is the voice of God.

CHAPTER II

The Founders of Irish Sanctity

There is a story of long standing in Ireland, which concerns one of the faithful who brought her newly-born daughter for Baptism. She informed the Priest that she had chosen for the child the name Hazel. The Priest was outraged, because, as he said, there is a saint for every day of the year, and no Irish woman should be asked to go through life, called after a nut.

To be sure, Ireland, in terms of numbers of its saints suffers from what the French call "un embarras de richesses." Anybody who has tried to construct a calendar of Irish saints has found a problem in choosing only one name for some days from a variety of saints who share it. A related problem arises for those who seek the starting point in any study which purports to be a history of Irish sanctity.

St. Patrick did not institute the beginnings of Christianity in Ireland. Nor was he the first of her traditional Saints. Allowing for a natural lack of precise records of those early times, it can be said with reasonable certainty that the first Irish Saint lived more than two centuries before the birth of Patrick. A feature of the group who preceded Patrick is that so many of them established their cult outside Ireland.

There are only five canonised Irish saints, who will be described in due course, as will those who have been acknowledged at various times and in various ways by individual Popes. Irish people whose Causes are presently under investigation will also be mentioned. All this is in chronological order, which inevitably means that popular or traditional saints will be those who occupy the scene until the story comes to the point at which an Irish saint was canonised.

Many Irish people are still surprised to hear that most great Irish saints were never canonised. A still greater surprise to them is that Patrick was not the first saint in Irish history. Perhaps most surprising of all to some people is the fact that Armagh is not the oldest See in Ireland. All these points and more will emerge on

14

these pages. We start with brief accounts of the oldest known Irish saints.

Abban (Abben) of Abingdon, England 2nd century
13 May

There are at least three Abbans among Irish saints. This one gave his name to the town of Abingdon in Berkshire, England, in the year 165. This town has sometimes been referred to as Abbendun, using, significantly, the Gaelic "dun". If his Irish origins can be accepted, he has the proud distinction of having been the first of a line of Irish saints stretching over more than eighteen centuries.

Gunifort of Pavia 303
26 August

One of the very earliest of Irish saints. He arrived in Germany with his brother, Gunibald, and two sisters. His sisters were martyred in Germany and Gunibald in Northern Italy, at Como. Gunifort managed to escape to Pavia where he died of wounds inflicted on his way to execution. His relics have been continuously venerated there, and Pavia later became a centre for Irish missioners. The Sacred Congregation of Rites officially established his feast day in 1914, fixing it on 26 August.

Mansuetus (Mansuy) of Toul, France 4th century
24 September

About the year 340, the Pope sent Mansuetus to be the first Bishop of Toul. A 10th century biographer states quite firmly that Mansuy came from Ireland.

Grimonia of Soissons, France 4th century
24 September

The town of La Chapelle grew round the church built to the memory of this Irish woman. She was martyred near Soissons, and miracles which followed her death led to her cult. The relics of Grimonia and her Irish companion, Proba, have been since the 16th century in the Abbey of Henin-Lietard, Douai, France.

Eliph of Toul, France c. 362
16 October

Julian, the Apostate, had this Irish monk beheaded at Toul, France. Eliph's brother, Eucharius, and two sisters were martyred with him. Mount Eliph, near Toul, commemorates this event. Their relics are now in Cologne.

Ailbhe of Emly, Co. Tipperary 5th century
12 September

This is the first of the four bishops Patrick found in Ireland. There seems no reason to doubt that all four had valid consecration as Bishops. Tradition has it that Ailbhe baptized David of Wales. Another tradition is that an angel showed Ailbhe the "place of his resurrection", Emly. For long the belief persisted that he had constant dialogue with angels, and constant guidance from them.

His name is said to be derived from the Gaelic words "ail-rock" and "beo-living". This is associated with the legend that he was abandoned as a baby and left under a stone, where a she-wolf found him and suckled him. He was rescued and grew up in a local family who gave him his name. More reliable than such a story, is the fact that his See of Emly is officially listed by the Vatican as being founded in the 4th century. This makes it many years older than Armagh and it has therefore, the distinction of being the oldest continuous See in Ireland.

Declan of Ardmore, Waterford 5th century
24 July

Declan is the second of the four bishops who were already working in Ireland, when Patrick arrived. Tradition has it that he had a bell which worked miracles, called the Duibhin Declain, and that this bell came down to him from heaven while he was celebrating Mass. The legend goes on that Declan led a group of Irish monks on a visit to Wales, at the end of which they left without the bell. In response to Declan's prayer, the stone or boulder, on which he had left the bell, floated out to them as they waited in their boat.

Declan is an outstanding example of an ancient Saint whose cult has not only survived, but has recently shown a marked revival. This is demonstrated mostly by a renewed interest in pilgrimages to his well at Tool, in Munster.

Ibar of Beg-Eri, Wexford c. 499
23 April

This was the bishop who showed most reluctance to accept the authority of Patrick. His reason was that Patrick was not Irish. He gave way in the end, thus making Patrick's task somewhat easier. The devotion to Ibar on his island in Wexford Harbour was quite extraordinary and drew the attention of English agents of the Reformation, who regarded it as important to stamp out this cult.

It was one of those who, in the 17th century, described the hold of this devotion on the people and the legends surrounding the wooden image of St. Ibar in his little chapel. According to this account, many attempts were made to burn this image, which was always restored to its proper place quite intact.

Kieran (Ciaran) of Saigher, Co. Offaly   5th century
5 March

The Feast of Kieran, the fourth of these bishops, is celebrated in all the Dioceses of Ireland. He was prepared for the priesthood at Tours, probably in the great Abbey of Marmoutier, famous for its founder, St. Martin. It is believed by some authorities that Kieran is the same person as St. Piran, the well-known Cornish saint who shares his feast day. At Saigher, he founded not only a monastery, but also a convent. It is worth noting that those who hold that Brigid founded the first convent for women in Ireland have not taken into account this convent of Kieran at Saigher, which must have preceded Brigid's foundation at Kildare by many years.

Patrick, the Apostle of Ireland   387–465
17 March

"For having annexed Ireland to the Kingdom of God, amid so many sufferings and tribulations, with unrivalled Christian heroism, his people have honoured and blessed him throughout the ages, as has been the case with no other national apostle." Such was the judgement of Dom Louis Gougard, one of the many Benedictine monks who have done so much to establish the prestige of the Saints of the Golden Age of Ireland.

A modern Irish historian commented whimsically that Patrick has confused his own story for posterity, and that historians have been confusing it ever since. In his Confession and his Letter to Coroticus, Patrick has told us a little, but not enough, about his family or place of birth. Still more important, perhaps, is the fact that he has given no clear information about the twenty years or so which elapsed between his escape from capitivity in Ireland and his return as Apostle. As a result, a great mass of literature has been produced that is full of learned speculation on the facts of his personal history.

It is accepted that he was a Celt but not a Gael. It is also accepted that his name was Sucat, not Patricius, which was the old Roman title of nobility, still bestowed by Popes at that time. It is also accepted that he was a captive in Ireland in his boyhood for some six years. It was at the end of this period that the legend of Patrick really begins. His escape began with his conviction that "voices" were calling him to return to his fatherland. His great destiny began then, for at a later date, other "voices" from Ireland compelled him to "come back and walk once more among us." Thus arose one of the great traditions of Ireland "The Voice of the Irish". When Pope John Paul II set foot on Irish soil in 1979, almost his first words to the Irish people were that he too, like Patrick, had come to the Irish. He too had heard the "Voice of the Irish".

So much has been written about Patrick's place in history, that details of the universal cult associated with him tend to be forgotten. Yet, at the very beginning of his Mission, he initiated two traditions centred on symbols which he chose – the shamrock to illustrate the Trinity, and by lighting the fire at Tara he initiated the tradition that the fire of Christ would never be extinguished in Ireland.

The cult of Patrick began in France, long before he received the title of Patricius, which was immediately prior to his departure on his Mission and probably in 431. The centre of the cult is a few miles west of Tours, on the river Loire, around the town of St. Patrice which is named after him. The legend is very strong and very persistent in that locality that Patrick not only spent the years there between his escape and the start of his Mission, but that his home was there – the fatherland to which the "voices" summoned him. It is the people of this area who most firmly believe that he was the nephew of St. Martin of Tours and that he became a monk in St. Martin's great Abbey of Marmoutier.

This cult goes back to the legend of Les Fleurs de St. Patrice – The Flowers of St. Patrick. According to this story, Patrick was sent from the Abbey to preach the Gospel in the area of Bréhémont on the river Loire. He went fishing one day and had an abnormal catch. The fishermen of the area were incensed and forced him to flee. He reached the north bank and sheltered and slept under a blackthorn bush. When he awoke the bush was covered in flowers. Since this was Christmas Day, this incident was a phenomenon, interpreted as a miracle, which was repeated on Christmas Day regularly until the bush was destroyed in World War I. Indeed, this phenomenon was tested many times and verified by various observers, including official organisations.

The cult began immediately and became firmly established when news trickled back that "their" monk had become the Apostle of Ireland. He is now the Patron of the fishermen on the Loire and, according to a modern French scholar, the Patron of almost every other occupation in the neighbourhood. There is a grotto dedicated to him at the Abbey which contains a stone bed, alleged to be his. Patrick, incidentally, is a common Christian name among Frenchmen.

The level to which the Irish have raised the sanctity of Patrick can be judged by the fact that his name occurs in the most usual form of salutation in the gaelic language of Ireland, and in the English translation more commonly used. The standard expression is, "May God, Mary and Patrick bless you". His name occurs widely in prayers and blessings throughout Ireland.

Among the oldest devotions of Ireland is the prayer used by travellers invoking the protection of Patrick, An Mhairbhne Phaidriac, The Elegy of Patrick. Another tradition has it that the date of his Feast, 17 March, ends the winter. He is alleged to have promised prosperity to those who seek his intercession on that day. A particularly attractive and persistent legend is that the Peace of Christ will reign over all Ireland when the Palm and the Shamrock meet, which means when St. Patrick's Day falls on Palm Sunday.

The continuity of devotion to Patrick is assured by the continued tradition of pilgrimages to Croagh Patrick and Lough Derg. There are very few people in Ireland who have never been to one or other of those during their lifetime. The fame of Lough Derg has been firmly established outside Ireland by a number of foreign writers. The most notable example is "El Purgatorio de San Patricio", a play written by the famous Spanish dramatist, Calderon.

There is no national Apostle so closely associated with the people as St. Patrick is with the Irish. His is the commonest name given to their Churches throughout the world. There is, in fact, a St. Patrick's Church in Rome. The annual processions on St. Patrick's Day in America are the greatest demonstrations of their kind in the world. On that day in 1932, the fifteenth centenary of his arrival in Ireland as Apostle, the Mass at the Eucharistic Congress assembled the largest gathering of Irish people possibly in the history of Ireland up to that time. More recently, in 1979, this was surpassed when Pope Paul II, following, as he said, in the footsteps of Patrick, celebrated Mass in Dublin before what may have been the largest congregation in the history of the Catholic Church.

The guidebooks of Italy refer to an unusual dedication to him there. It is called the "Well of St. Patrick", at Orvieto. It is exceptionally deep, with 248 steps from the surface to the Well. It was built at the orders of Pope Clement VII to provide water for the city during its periodic sieges, and was completed in 1537. The connection with St. Patrick arises because the project was carried out by a member of the Sangallo family which derives its name from the Irish St. Gall (see p. 46). As a result the completed project was dedicated to the Irish Apostle by the builder, Sangallo. A very common proverb in Italian now perpetuates the tradition. According to this, big spenders are said to have pockets "as deep as the Well of St. Patrick".

Finally, the *Lorica*, or Breastplate of St. Patrick, is a literary treasure of Ireland. It is alleged to be the invocation which led him and his party safely to the confrontation with the High King and the Druids at Tara at the beginning of the Mission. In Irish, the Breastplate is known as the Faeth Fiadha, the Deer's Cry. This name is based on the legend that Patrick and his eight companions, on their way to confront the Ard-Ri, the High King at Tara, were miraculously changed into deer, so avoiding the attentions of the King's guards sent to intercept them and prevent their arrival at Tara.

> Christ be with me, Christ be before me:
> Christ be behind me, Christ be with me:
> Christ be beneath me, Christ be above me:
> Christ be at my right, Christ be at my left:
> Christ be in the fort, Christ be in the chariot:
> Christ be in the ship.
> Christ be in the heart of everyone who thinks of me:
> Christ be in the mouth of everyone who speaks to me:
> Christ be in every eye that sees me;
> Christ be in every ear that hears me.

Brigid of Kildare   452–524
1 February

In the whole story of the conversion of Ireland and the long episode of missionary and scholarly activity which followed, the status of Brigid, or Bride, is unique. She never left Ireland, yet she is venerated over the whole world. She was the real prototype of all nuns. She bridged the gap, more clearly than any other, between the Christian and the pagan cultures. In England, there are nineteen dedications to her, the most important of which is the oldest place of Christian worship in London, St. Bride's in Fleet Street, as well as the Bridewell, originally St. Bride's Well. St. Thomas à Becket was born in that parish, and it is said that Cardinal Wolsey was one of its priests.

She was born about 462, the year in which Patrick founded the first of the Schools in Armagh. There is no clear evidence that Brigid ever met Patrick. It is, however, accepted that she founded what is said to have been the second of the Irish Schools, at Kildare. This was not one, but two foundations, one for men, the other for women, and she installed there a bishop, Conlaeth. The Vatican officially lists the See of Kildare as dating from 519.

Kildare, or Cill Daire, the Church of the Oak, was unique in Ireland because of its dual character. The oak was sacred to the druids, and in the inner sanctuary of the Church was permanently maintained the sacred fire, a religious symbol of the druid faith. This fire was not finally extinguished until the dissolution of the monasteries during the Reformation.

All those features have led some historians to speculate that Brigid was the high priestess of a community of druid women, and that she led the entire community into the Christian faith, and christianised its monuments. Such a feat, if true, indicates something of the enormous dynamic quality of Brigid and would explain her obvious sway over her own and succeeding generations.

There is a school of thought which maintains that the knights of the Middle Ages, who looked for Madonna-like qualities in their womenfolk, chose Brigid as their model. Such was her image according to this theory, and so closely did this image correspond to their ideal that the word "bride" passed into the English language, based on this image. Linguistic experts, however, prefer to believe that the expression derives from the old German "bryd" or "bride". In 1283, three knights took with them the head of Brigid on a journey to the Holy Land. They met their death in Lumier, near Lisbon. The Church at Lumier now has her head enshrined in a special chapel dedicated to Brigid.

Devotion to her is widespread in Scotland. East and West Kilbride, not far from Glasgow, bear her name. St Brigid's Church at Douglas commemorates the fact that she is a patroness of the great Douglas family. More than twenty places on the west coast alone are dedicated to her. It is also recorded that, after the defeat of Harold, the last Anglo-Saxon King of England, his sister fled to Belgium taking with her the cloak of Brigid, which is now one of the sacred treasures of the cathedral at Bruges.

It was commonplace for Irish missionaries to initiate devotion to Brigid in their territories, so her name appears in breviaries, litanies and missals in all the countries of western Europe. The Irish Saint Donato, Bishop of Fiesole in Italy, built St. Brigid's Church in Piacenza 1100 years ago. It was in this Church in 1185 that the Peace of Constance was ratified. It was declared a national monument in Italy in 1911. The Brigidine Nuns, founded in 1807, are now a worldwide Order.

The best-known of the customs connected with Brigid is the plaiting of rush crosses for St. Brigid's feast day. This tradition goes back to the story that she was plaiting rush crosses while nursing a dying pagan chieftain. He asked her about this and her explanation led to his being baptised. There are many devotions and prayers dedicated to her. Her name used to figure in Gaelic sayings, in the same way as Patrick, in the expression "Brid agus Muire dhuit – Brigid and Mary be with you." Even in Welsh, an invocation used by travellers calls on Brigid "Sanffried suynade ni undeith – St. Brigid bless us on our journey." In the western Isles of Scotland, she is mentioned in a blessing to be said over the cattle in the morning, "The protection of God and Colmkille encompass your going and coming, and about you be the milk-maid of the smooth white palms, Brigid of the clustering, golden brown hair." Finally, the name Brigid has over the centuries been the favourite name for Irish girls second only to Mary, and the number of French boys given the name of Patrick or Patrice is equalled by the frequency of Brigid or Brigitte among French girls.

All the evidence shows that she was, at the least, an exceptional personality, a woman chosen for an unusual destiny. She infected by her enthusiasm all those who came into contact with her, and the cult which sprang up around her has spread far and wide and lasted for fourteen centuries. Posterity has found it an insoluble problem to decide who has been the greatest of all Irishmen. It has never had any doubt who has been the greatest of all Irish women. This is why Brigid is known as the Mary of the Gaels.

CHAPTER III

The Golden Age of Ireland

"Ireland had become the heiress to the classical and theological learning of the western empire of the fourth and fifth centuries, and a period of humanism was thus ushered in which reached its culmination during the sixth and the following centuries. For once, at any rate, Ireland drew upon herself the eyes of the world, as the one haven of rest in a turbulent world overrun by hordes of barbarians, as the great seminary of Christian and classical learning. Her sons, carrying Christianity and a new humanism over Great Britain and the Continent, became the teachers of whole nations, the counsellors of kings and emperors."

(Kuno Meyer, *Ancient Irish Poetry*)

It was a French scholar, Arsène Darmstetter, who recorded the judgement that the Renaissance began, not in Italy, in the twelfth century, but in Ireland seven centuries earlier. In 1844, German scholars presented to Daniel O'Connell an Address in which they declared the debt their country owed to Ireland, whose sons rescued Germany from paganism and ignorance. An Italian authority, Negri, stated categorically that European poetry owes the origin of rhyme to the Irish tradition.

In reading the comments of foreign writers, one is led inevitably to the conclusion that Ireland could claim to have saved civilisation after the fall of the Roman Empire, or at least to have played a major role in that process. It is worth a comment that such an opinion is not based on the writings of Irishmen, but of foreign scholars. The list of these is impressive by any standards. Many of them made a career of the study of Irish scholarly activities. More than one, like Kuno Meyer, quoted above, actually made Ireland the base of their studies, and their home for many years. The period loosely described as the Golden Age of Ireland is generally said to have begun about a century after the mission of St. Patrick. It is almost normally held to have finished with the Viking invasions of Ireland in the ninth and tenth centuries. It would be more accurate to say that the Viking raids seriously affected the work of the schools which continued on a very much reduced scale. Those who say the Golden Age was ended by the havoc of the Vikings, would have to account for the fact that the greatest scholar Ireland ever sent to Europe was trained after the Viking terror had already started. Strangely enough, he bore the most Irish name of any of the illustrious company, John Scotus Eriugena, John the Scot from Ireland. Again those who would have it that Irish missionary activity ended with the Vikings, overlook the fact that half a century after Brian Boru put an end to the Viking power in Ireland at the battle of Clontarf in 1014, an Irish monk established one of the greatest congregations of Irish Abbeys in the whole history of the Golden Age. This was Marianus of Ratisbon.

Clearly there are elements in this story which should be clarified, and this study is intended to do that. It is also intended to place the achievements of great figures of the Golden Age of Ireland more firmly in the context of the modern age. The Ireland of today is part of a unique generation, one which has grown up at a time of upheaval in social development throughout the world. In that situation, it is easy to conclude that the work of Irishmen of the Middle Ages, interesting and useful, and even glorious at the time, is now part of a history which has come to an end. A second look at all this must compel a revision of such a judgement. Modern attitudes to social problems lead the superficial observer to conclude that what the old Irish missioners had to and did contribute, was entirely within the context of a growing society, long past and in no way related to the present day.

The modern generation of Irishmen live in a society which seems somewhat divorced from the institutions of the past. Among these inevitably is the Church. So to add to a certain lack of interest in the events of the Golden Age, the impression can grow that Irish saints and even scholars were ascetic by nature and remote from the social needs of contemporary society. These notes have tried to stress in the selection of names, those who left after them a strong debt from the society in which they lived. Such were Dymphna of Gheel, Fiacre of Meaux and others.

Quite suddenly, mankind has begun to accept as public responsibilities what for centuries formed the basis of voluntary charity. The care of the mentally afflicted, for example, is now increasingly accepted as a responsibility of government, in place of the universal neglect and even hostility such affliction received for centuries. Throughout all those centuries, the image of the

Irish Saint Dymphna inspired the town of Gheel in Belgium to treat with compassion the mentally sick who, everywhere else, were outcasts in society. Irish saints were the forerunners of every kind of social activity. The care of the sick and the old, accepted as God's work, goes back to Brigid of Kildare and probably before her in the Christian tradition of Ireland. In France, the most famous patron of the sick, St. Vincent de Paul, regarded the Irish monk, Fiacre of Meaux, as his model. Throughout Europe, the veneration of Irish Saints is often based on their obvious sanctity, but also on the positive contribution they made, not only to the society of their time, but in anticipation of the permanent needs of mankind and in advance of modern thought.

In dealing with selected examples of Irish missionaries who contributed most obviously, either to the Christian world as a whole or to Ireland as their country, one purpose will be served and that is to make Irishmen aware of this great Irish image from the universal aspect of contributions to mankind. It is a curious feature of the story that foreign communities are often more aware of the real contributions of Irish missionaries than the Irish people to whom these saintly men belonged. Great Irishmen in impressive numbers are venerated all over Western Europe and too often ignored in Ireland. In many cases, their Irishness is accepted by their devotees abroad and disputed by their own people. Such are Dymphna of Gheel and Fridolin of Switzerland. Ironically enough, Fridolin is probably the only Irish saint in Europe on whose feast-day the Irish flag is flown, outside Ireland, in Europe.

From the point of view of Ireland itself, it would be easy to say that any Irish who left Ireland as "exiles for Christ" had ceased to contribute anything to Ireland. This would be a vast mis-statement and a grave injustice to all these people. Those who think along those lines have forgotten how many great abbeys and hospices in Europe were reserved entirely for Irish monks. They have forgotten also that the whole basis of Irish culture was firmly built into Irish history more by Columba of Iona than by any other single Irishman.

It is worth repeating that no Irish leader outside Holy Orders ever succeeded in creating a national image until perhaps Brian Boru partially achieved this at the Battle of Clontarf. By contrast, every missionary who left Ireland for Europe was accepted as an Irishman without regard to his local associations at home. In Ireland itself, local attachments and loyalties were a dominant feature of Irish society.

25

The age of the Saints and Scholars is said to have begun with the departure of Colmcille for Alba, as Scotland was called in the gaelic tradition. It is convenient in reviews of the period to accept this starting point, although on closer examination it is clear that Irish missioners and scholars had been known outside Ireland many years before Columba, and even before Patrick.

Perhaps the greatest permanent effect of the Golden Age of Ireland is the missionary tradition it left with the Irish people. While this, of course, was primarily directed towards the advancement of the Universal Church, the effects of it have been felt in every society. It has always been a feature of Irish missions to undertake tasks of positive value to mankind. Whole Orders of Irish priests, brothers and nuns have been founded with specific roles in society and often no other body exists to carry out such activities. Such Orders are the Sisters of Mercy, the Presentation Brothers and Sisters, the Irish Christian Brothers. In other cases, Irish people have joined Orders based elsewhere and are amongst their most prominent members. This is especially true in the English-speaking world, notably in the USA. It has become almost the custom there to expect Irish names to predominate amongst the Hierarchy and the clergy in general.

Hospitals and clinics founded and staffed by Irish personnel are commonplace throughout the world. In emerging countries, particularly in Africa, both primary and secondary education is strongly sustained by Irish religious. All this is a permanent result of the missionary tradition founded by the monks and nuns of Ireland who launched the Golden Age.

That, however, is part of a continuing story. Here the interest is in the major impact of Columba and those who followed. So it is accepted that Alba was the first of the territories which attracted the men of the Golden Age. From there, Irish monks played important roles in the conversion of England. France became a major field for their labours, so did the Low Countries. Germany and Switzerland followed, while the north of Italy has strong relics of Irish missionary and scholarly labours. The series opens with the Scottish Mission set up, appropriately, by the Apostle of the Gaels, Columba of Iona.

Saint Columba of Iona   521–597
9 June

The Apostle of the Gaels, Colm or Colmcille, from Gartan, Donegal, was the most illustrious member of the greatest family in

Irish history. That history, indeed, might have taken a very different course had he chosen to do what so many of his contemporaries would have wished, become King of Ulster and in turn High King of Ireland. Colmcille may well have been the greatest leader Ireland has ever produced. In Ireland itself, his intervention at the convention at Drumceat, near Limavady, in Ulster, effectively swung the nation away from its declared intention to suppress the Bardic Order. Colmcille persuaded all and sundry that the whole future of Gaelic culture demanded that the scholarship of the Bards should be preserved and his prestige was such that his views prevailed. He was an O'Neill, the great grandson of the Chieftain who brought St. Patrick to Ireland as a slave. By the time Colmcille finished his life's work, he had ensured that this family produced some of the greatest missioners who ever toiled for the Church inside or outside of Ireland.

In his chosen career as a monk, he had the most complete education Ireland had to offer. He studied under Finian of Moville, Finian of Clonard and Mobhi of Glasnevin. He acquired the Bardic skills and the traditional music of Ireland in the Bardic School of Gemman. He founded his first church schools in Derry. In quick succession, he established Durrow followed by Kells. This last was to achieve eternal fame when, in 807 the monks of Iona fled there from the Viking terror and completed the Book of Kells. After Kells, Colmcille founded Swords as well as some 40 churches and other schools in Ireland. All this was achieved by the time he was forty-two years of age and represented a level of success which assured for him a distinguished place in history. At that point, he decided to become an "exile for Christ" and chose as his mission territory the small area in the west coast of Scotland, peopled by his own Gaelic people who had formed what at the time was an Irish colony, which started out as a small group of emigrants from the North East corner of Ireland.

The success of Colmcille in this mission was enormous and destined to have a permanent effect on the future history of Scotland. It is strongly suggested in commentaries throughout the ages that the personal image of Columba as he was known there was the major influence in the rise of Gaelic power in Scotland. When he arrived, the ruling power in Scotland was the Pictish Kingdom. Little more than two centuries later, a Gael became King of all Scotland and the Picts had virtually disappeared as a significant element in Scottish life. Whether Colmcille intended this, or even foresaw it, is hard to determine. The situation as he found it in Scotland made it a possibility from the start that his presence would put unity and purpose into the entire Gaelic people. They saw in him a leader, an O'Neill of the race of Ulster Kings. In Irish terms, it cannot be overlooked that the Gaels of Scotland were from the beginning primarily Gaels of Ulster and as such accepted Colmcille as one of their own.

Colmcille did not come to convert the Picts, although he had to come to terms with their King Brude before he could conduct a mission. In fact, another Ulsterman, Moluag, had set up his mission at Lismore, on the west coast of Scotland about a year before Colmcille arrived, and it was he who concentrated on the Picts. The constant references to rivalry between these two over spheres of missionary influence are probably without foundation. Events seem to bear out the fact that Columba was primarily interested in every aspect of the Gaelic life in Scotland. Legends which suggest that he was in fact exiled to Scotland as a penance for grave errors are also doubtful. The most serious charge was that he invoked the military aid of his kinsmen against the High King, and caused the slaughter which took place at the Battle of Cul Dremne. The fact that he returned to Ireland several times, notably for the Convention of Drumceat, where his eloquence saved the Bards, is in no way consistent with such an exile or such legends.

His headquarters were set up at Iona, destined to become one of the most famous of the early missions of the Church. It was from here that the ultimate conversion of Scotland developed, although this final triumph only came with the elimination of the Picts. Iona was the centre which provided the greatest impetus in the conversion of England. In the eyes of the Church of Rome, Iona came to be known as the stronghold of resistance to conformity in certain practices of importance at the time. The major issue was the date of Easter, on which the monks of Iona and, incidentally, for a long time, the establishments in Ireland set up by Columba, were reluctant to agree. It was more than two centuries after the death of Columba before Rome's rulings were finally accepted.

His personal life and austerity set a standard which was a shining example to his monks. As a result, they established churches and monasteries on a scale seldom if ever equalled. He laboured for thirty-four years and when he died he had ensured the conversion of all the Gaels of Scotland. Nor should it be assumed that his monks were aloof from the Picts. Indeed, there is probably no territory developed by an Irish Mission where place names reflect the presence of Irish missionaries more than Scotland. A surprising example of this, probably not associated with Colmcille or Iona, is the capital city of Edinburgh. A leading Scottish authority on Celtic Scotland, W. F. Skene, holds the view that the original source of the name was an Irish nun Edana or Modenna, who established a community of nuns there. This ancient tradition is embodied in the expression Maiden Castle, associated with the earliest history of the city. The old name, Dunedin, was changed to Edinburgh allegedly in honour of the Anglo-Saxon King Edwin but that is clearly not the original name. In fact, the *Encyclopedia Britannica* discounts the theory that the name is in any way associated with Edwin.

One of the famous books connected with Colmcille is the Psaltair he is said to have copied in the monastery of Finian of Moville. This book was traditionally the Battle Book of the O'Donnells, his kinsmen, who carried it into battle. The hereditary keepers of the Cathach of St. Columba, later known as the Battle Book, were the family of the MacRobartaigh. Five centuries after the death of Colmcille, a member of this family, Muiredach Mac-Robartaigh, whose name in religion was Marianus Scotus, founded the Irish Abbey of Ratisbon which, in due course, became the Mother House of twelve Irish Abbeys on the Continent.

This Psaltair is the basis of one of the most famous of the legends connected with the Saint. According to this, he copied it from the original which belonged to Finian of Moville. Finian demanded both the original and the copy. Colmcille refused to part with the copy and in due course the dispute was brought before the Ard Ri, the High King, for judgement. Diarmuid, the Ard Ri, decided against Colmcille in words which have become proverbial in the Irish language – le gach buin a laogh; to every cow its calf.

Colmcille has been described as a poet, statesman, scholar, patriot and missionary. It is hard to know which role he would have claimed as his aim in life. He is honoured by all Scotland. Not even the Reformation caused his image to fade, and he is generally revered as the founder of the Scottish nation. Perhaps it is even more significant that he is the Patron of the powerful Catholic lay organisation, the Knights of St. Columba. This body serves both Scotland and England. The selection of St. Columba as Patron indicates the veneration in which he is held in both countries.

This organisation has been set up in various parts of the world. In each case different titles have been adopted. In Ireland, it is the Knights of St. Columbanus. In the USA, it is the Knights of Columbus, in South Africa the Knights of Da Gama, in West Africa the Knights of St. Mulumba, in Australia and New Zealand the Knights of the Southern Cross.

The prophecies of St. Malachy concerning the succession of Popes are universally known. The prophecies of St. Colmcille are no less remarkable. The publication in 1969 of *The Prophecies of St. Malachy and St. Columbkille** by Peter Bander has stirred a renewed interest in the prophecies of St. Colmcille. The account of the prophecies of St. Colmcille is, as might be expected, a progressive series of predictions of the whole future of his beloved country, Ireland, and seems to contain references right up to the present day.

The devotion to Colmcille is traditionally strongest in his own favourite city of Derry and so it has been for fourteen centuries. It is, therefore, not surprising that an astonishing event on 13th April in Derry was attributed to the intercession of their own Colmcille. This was the day of the signing by the King in London of the Catholic Emancipation Act. On that day, the statue of a Protestant leader of the siege of Derry, which stood on the Walls of Derry, suddenly broke apart. The upraised sword, for no reason that has ever been ascertained, crashed and smashed to pieces. The news of this spread through the entire world, coupled with the explanation held throughout the Catholic population, that it had been brought about by Saint Colmcille.

An ancient account has it that he left to Iona his stainless grace, to Derry his soul, and to Down his body. To Scotland, he left a Gaelic dynasty and nationhood. He was the greatest of the Gaels and the true Patron of Gaeldom. It is entirely appropriate, therefore, and consistent with that noble status, that it was he who, in his passionate defense of the Bardic Order of Ireland, coined the phrase which motivated every missioner and scholar of the Golden Age:

> Do chum gloire De, agus onora na hEirean
> To the glory of God and the honour of Ireland

Moluag (Lua, Molua) of Lismore, Scotland 530–592
25 June

It is almost customary in accounts of Moluag to quote the observation of Bernard of Clairvaux in his biography of St. Malachy. In this St. Bernard refers to the monk Luanus, identified as Lua, or Molua, or Moluag, a monk of Bangor, as having

* 4th edition 1979, Colin Smythe, Gerrards Cross, Bucks.

been the founder of 100 monasteries in Scotland. In fact Moluag took rank as a missioner alongside Columba, or Colmcille. In general terms, Moluag was the apostle of the Picts, while Columba was the Apostle of the Gaels.

Beyond the fact that he was educated at the schools of Bangor, not much is known in detail of his origins, though it is generally understood that he, like Colmcille, is an Ulsterman. Whether he was an O'Neill is not clear but since noble birth was almost normal with early missionaries, it can be assumed in the case of Moluag. In his mission it seems that, either by mutual agreement, or by the wish of the Pictish King Brude, or by mere chance, Moluag largely confined his missionary efforts to the Picts of the east and Colmcille to the Gaelic kingdom.

Inevitably, legends have grown over the centuries according to which there was bitter rivalry between these two. It would be realistic to dismiss this as being quite inconsistent with the level of dedication and achievement of these two great missionaries. The events seem to bear out the fact that substantially they worked among two distinct national groups. In modern times historical accounts of events at that time quite often allot all the credit in the Scottish missions to Colmcille. In fact the Bishopric of Argyle and the Isles was awarded not to Colmcille's Iona, but to Moluag's Lismore. The blackthorn crozier of Moluag, his Bachuill Mor, is in the possession of the Campbells, Dukes of Argyle, who traditionally carried it with them into battle.

Moluag, for some reasons connected with legendary miracles has a strong tradition of protection against insanity. On the island of Lewis, the custom persisted right up to the nineteenth century of conducting a ritual service of intercession to Moluag at his titular church Teampall Mo Luigh. It was also the custom to pray for his intercession in the cure of wounds and to send wooden replicas of the cured limbs. This widespread devotion to Moluag was a source of considerable irritation to Scottish reformers who strove incessantly to stamp it out.

Moluag actually arrived about a year before Colmcille in Scotland. He was accompanied by Comgall, an Irish Pict, who presented him to King Brude to obtain his authority for the mission. Colmcille, incidentally, got Comgall to perform exactly the same service for him. It is quite possible that King Brude preferred Moluag to Colmcille, and that is what led Moluag to concentrate rather more on the Picts. It would be quite natural that the Pictish King might have some reservation about the Ulster Prince Colmcille who was a natural leader of the Gaelic people in

Scotland. However that may be, the presence of the two Irish missionaries gradually brought to an end the armed conflict between the two nations.

A Scottish King, Malcolm II, defeated the Vikings in 1010 at the town of Murlach, named after Moluag. As a memorial he built there an Abbey, a Cathedral and a Bishop's See. The Scottish See at Lismore was still the See of Argyll until the approach of the Reformation. By that time the decline of the image of Moluag had gone side by side with the rise of the Gaelic influence in Scotland.

This decline is quite simply explained. The result of Colmcille's labours among the Gaels was an expansion of their influence and a corresponding decline of Pictish power. From being a colony of Ireland, the Gaelic settlement became a Gaelic kingdom. Indeed Colmcille carried out the first Christian inauguration in history of a King when he consecrated Aidan, as King of the Scots, thus instituting an Irish dynasty. In due course, his descendant Kenneth MacAlpine became the first Irish King of Scotland and the line died with the death of Alexander III in 1286. All this was accompanied by the disappearance, as a power, of the Picts and, as a consequence, the status of Moluag, the Apostle of the Picts, has been diminished.

There are, however, many memorials to him in the form of ancient churches and placenames. Kilmoluag is a common example. So is Murlach. A leading authority on the Celtic Church in Scotland states that the Gaelic names for a whole series of old church sites, stretching right through the Great Glen, all bear the name of Moluag. The name Luke, which is quite common among men in Scotland, is reliably stated to be derived from Moluag.

Aiden of Lindisfarne   651
31 August

In 634, Oswald assumed the throne of Northumbria and began a reign which was to have a profound and lasting effect on the conversion of England and to leave to posterity the image of a saint. He had lived in exile among Irish monks at Iona and on his return decided to entrust to them the conversion of his kingdom. The first missioner, Corman, was unsuccessful and Aidan was sent in his place and established as a bishop in Lindisfarne. A unique feature of Aidan's apostolate was that his message was conveyed in Irish and the main interpreter was King Oswald. Some sources insist that at this time Irish was the language of Oswald's court, a somewhat unlikely situation. Oswald was killed in battle by the pagan Penda in 642, and from then until his death in 651 Aidan worked with Oswald's successor, Oswin. The greatest tribute to the work of Aidan must be the effect he had on the two monarchs whose names have lived on as popular saints in England.

The Venerable Bede, whose writings record the greatest respect and gratitude for the work done by Irish missioners for his Anglo-Saxon people, had special praise for Aidan. These tributes to Irish monks were all the more noteworthy since Bede had to record, with deep sorrow, the almost total absence of missioners from among British Celts, notably in Wales. This was due to resentment over certain incidents concerned with military oppression which Anglo-Saxon warriors had inflicted on Celts in Britain. One interesting and quite long-lasting effect of the establishment of Aidan's communities of Irish monks was that the education of Anglo-Saxons was carried out by Irish teachers. As a result, it is said that for many years English writing was distinguished by its Irish lettering.

Aidan was one of the Irish monks who did not adhere to the Roman ruling on Easter. It was the Irish tradition to observe a fixed Easter and for a long time the Irish Church declined to conform to the Roman rule. In fact, Iona was probably the last stronghold of this resistance in the whole Church. Ironically enough, it was an Anglo-Saxon monk at Iona, Egbert, who finally persuaded the community to conform in 729. Bede describes how this difference of opinion with Aidan caused him great regret but in no way altered his great respect for him. One custom of Aidan became general in Ireland, and is in fact embodied in the Irish language in an important way. It was he who brought into his establishments the fast on Wednesday and Friday, and brought into the Irish language the words for Wednesday, Ceadaon, first fast, and for Friday, dia hAoine, the main fast.

It now seems to be the general opinion that Aidan was the real apostle of England. Augustine, who was destined by the Pope for that role, had insuperable problems, well described by the Venerable Bede. As a result, his real impact was in the South-East, principally in Kent. In the event, it was Aidan and other Irish monks who effectively converted England.

A nineteenth century Anglican Bishop of Durham and historian, Dr. Lightfoot, states that Augustine was the apostle of Kent, but Aidan was the apostle of England. Still later, in 1951, the Anglican Bishop Hudson, speaking at the 1300th anniversary of Aidan's death used the words, "Blessed Aidan, apostle of Northumberland, yes and of England."

Colman of Lindisfarne 676

18 February

Colman became the third Irish Abbot of Lindisfarne in succession on the death of Finian in 661. He was called upon to defend the Irish position on the vexed question of the date of Easter at the Synod of Whitby in 663. Having lost the battle at the Synod he resigned and returned to Ireland.

The importance to the Catholic Church of establishing agreement on the observance of Easter at the same time in the whole Church should not be minimized. The whole liturgical year revolves around the date of Easter, just as the Resurrection is at the very root of the Christian faith. There were at least three methods of calculating the date, all supported to a greater or lesser extent by historical arguments. In 525 Rome decided to institute a new enquiry and about the year 600 adopted the date fixed by this. By about 632 most of Ireland had fallen in line.

Columba of Iona had strongly held to the old Irish tradition. His prestige was such that his example was followed not only by all those associated with Iona, but virtually all of Ulster and even monasteries and schools elsewhere in Ireland, with Columban traditions, such as Kells and Durrow. Since the Irish influence was so strong in England, and especially in the north of the country, King Oswy of Northumbria called a Council, historically known as the Synod of Whitby, in 663 to settle once and for all whether the Church in his territory would follow the Roman or the Irish practice.

The King ruled that the decision of the Synod was in favour of the Roman practice. Colman, unable to accept the ruling preferred to return to Ireland. There has always been considerable doubt whether the ruling of the Synod accurately represented the true verdict of those present. It seems that there was a distinct majority against change, and a strong suggestion of Anglo-Saxon pressures, led by Wilfred, who was well-known for his antipathy to all Irish practices. Moreover, there seems to have been considerable confusion since leading speakers had to make their points through interpreters. Lindisfarne, incidentally, retained its Irish influence, since Tuda, the next Abbot was Irish, but he was an adherent of the Roman calculation of the date of Easter.

Colman's reaction was not so much a refusal to accept change as a refusal to accept the King's ruling in a spiritual matter. In the event, he was accompanied on his return to Ireland by an unspecified number of Irish monks and about thirty Anglo-Saxons, a fair indication of strong support in his decision. Colman established the whole party in a new monastery at Innisboffin, an island off Connemara.

Not long after, the Anglo-Saxon contingent expressed great dissatisfaction on the grounds that they were not treated on equal terms by their Irish brethren. They complained of long absences on the part of the Irish monks and the unfair allocation of duties. There seems to have been some grounds for their dissatisfaction, for Colman decided to help the Anglo-Saxons set up their own monastery in Mayo. This unique establishment was to become famous as Mayo of the Saxons, the first Abbot being Gerald, alleged to have been the son of an Anglo-Saxon King. The monastery was still flourishing 900 years later, although by the nature of things its English character could not have lasted long after its foundation. It is said that the Bishop of Mayo, Patrick O'Healy, the Franciscan martyred in 1579, was associated with Mayo of the Saxons.

Saint Columbanus of Luxeuil   543–615
23 November

It has been noted over the years that the memory of St. Patrick suffered a decline in the gaelic society of Ireland for many centuries. This view is based largely on the fact that so few Irishmen seemed to have borne the name of Patrick until the great military leader, Patrick Sarsfield, brought it into favour twelve centuries after the death of Patrick. Historians have suggested that the alleged eclipse of Patrick was due to the fact that he was not Irish. A more likely reason is the world fame of those who followed him. Three, in particular, fall into that category; Brigid, the Mary of the Gaels, Colmcille or Columba, the Apostle of Scotland, and Columbanus. Columbanus was one of the earliest, and destined to be the greatest of the Celtic missionaries on the Continent. He was of a noble Leinster family and was a product of the famous schools of Bangor, Co. Down. He arrived in France about 575 accompanied, as so often was the case with missions, by twelve others on the model of the Apostles.

He laboured for thirty years and left the image of a determined, fearless, perhaps even arrogant, defender of faith and morals. He had no initial authority, yet he denounced kings for their loose morals and bishops for their complacency. More than once, he was the subject of complaints to the Holy See. In his letters to the Pope, he was very outspoken but quite definite in his submission to the authority of Rome. The real reason why he survived so many attacks was that he was regarded as the leading figure in the Celtic Church. There is no doubt that there was real fear at the time that the centre of Christendom might pass into the hands of the Celts. His letters to Rome, therefore, and his submission to the Supreme Pontiff, as the successor to Peter, is one of the most significant events, not only in the history of Ireland but in the history of the Church. He dedicated Ireland to the Universal Church, and laid to rest any fear that the Celtic Church was a threat to Rome. He also instituted the long tradition of devotion to the Papacy which is characteristic of the Irish Church. The response of the Irish people to the visit of Pope John Paul II in 1979 was consistent with that tradition.

Columbanus founded his first monastery at Annegray in 575. The interest it aroused compelled him to expand and in 590 he built the more famous abbey at Luxeuil and, two years later, another at Fontaines. In 610, the king of Burgundy, incensed at Columbanus' criticism of his way of life, banished Irish monks from the territory. In his wanderings, Columbanus founded one monastery after another, while his disciples were active on their own account. From this remarkable missionary effort arose over 100 monasteries in France and Switzerland. Among the most famous in France were Lure, Coutances, Faremoutiers, Jouarre, Reuil, Besançon. In Switzerland, one of the company founded the Abbey of Ursanne, another at Tuggen and another at Bregenz.

The two greatest monuments to the mission of Columbanus were St. Gall in Switzerland founded by his companion Gall, and Bobbio in Italy, founded by Columbanus himself. Bobbio was in its time probably the most famous abbey in Europe. It flourished for twelve centuries till Napoleon closed it in 1802. Its great library was then divided among various libraries in Europe. Pope Pius XI stated that the collection from Bobbio accounted for much of the prestige enjoyed among scholars by the Ambrosian Library in Milan.

The lasting influence of Columbanus can be gauged from the fact that in North East Italy alone, there are twenty-three parishes dedicated to him. In the USA, Bishop Edward J. Galvin, born in 1882, on 23 November, the feast day of Columbanus, founded the Columban Missionary Society in 1916, followed in 1922 by the Missionary Sisters of St. Columban.

Finally, when the greatest of the lay organisations of Ireland was set up, there was prolonged discussion as to the patron to whom it should be dedicated. Given the long list of illustrious Irishmen available for such selection, it is of special interest that they chose this outstanding missioner in foreign fields. So arose the Knights of St. Columbanus.

Fursa of Peronne 649
16 January

About the year 631, King Sigesbert of East Anglia welcomed into his territory an Irish priest from Galway, and invited him to found the monastery of Burghcastle in Suffolk. Some ten years later, this priest went on a pilgrimage to Rome. He never returned to England and became the centre of one of the most remarkable and persistent of all the cults in France.

He had already established his cult in England. The Venerable Bede wrote more extensively of Fursa than of any other Irish missionary except, of course, Aidan. The famous Visions of St. Fursa were known to Bede, and he more than any other authority esttablished the validity of this tradition, which launched Fursa into universal fame. Twelve centuries later, the famous English writer, Sir Francis Palgrave, in his History of Normandy and England, stated: "We have no difficulty in deducing the poetic genealogy of Dante's Inferno from the Milesian Fursaeus."

The impact of Fursa on all who met him was immense. Legends which attributed miracles to him during his own life-time are so numerous that he must be placed alongside the greatest saints in the entire history of the Church. He initiated his mission to France, it is said, by restoring to life the son of a local noble-man, who begged him to remain and build his monastery in his land. Instead he founded the Abbey of Peronne which became ever after Peronna Scotorum (Peronne of the Irish). He also founded one of the most famous Abbeys of France, Lagny, followed by St. Quentin.

It is not surprising that Fursa is held by many to have brought about more conversions than any other Irish missionary in France. His sanctity was a topic of conversation far and wide and came to the attention of French kings and nobles, who vied with each other to attract him to their territories. Perhaps the most remarkable feature of Fursa's story is that the possession of his remains was disputed by leading French rulers. It so happened that he died at Mazerolles. Now this happened to be the very place where he carried out the miracle, on his arrival, of restoring to life the son of the local nobleman, Count Haymon. Not unnaturally, the Count planned to have Fursa interred at Mazerolles but the Chancellor of Peronne, Erchinvald, sent a royal guard which summarily took possession of the body and bore it off to Peronne. For four years, the body lay in a portico awaiting the completion of a magnificent new Church to receive him. Bede records this event briefly in the words "concerning the incorruption of his body, we have briefly taken notice so that the sublime character of this man may be better known to the readers".

Fursa has, of course, special interest for all Irish people. His feast day is celebrated on 16th January throughout Ireland. It is also celebrated in the Diocese of Northampton in England. It is hard to believe, considering the universal nature of his cult, that Fursa founded one of the great Irish monastic traditions in Europe. His Abbey at Peronne was reserved for Irish monks, a tradition which grew and spread in monasteries all over Europe. Four centuries later, Marianus MacRobartaigh founded at Ratisbon the great congregation of Irish monasteries, twelve in all. The Irish character of these monasteries was confirmed by Bulls of Pope Innocent II and, in 1148, by Pope Eugenius.

Finally, to illustrate the enduring quality of the cult of Fursa, it is worth recalling the special interest shown by Louis IX, the Saint-King of France. He declared his desire to be present, in 1256, at the translation of the remains of Fursa to a new shrine at Peronne. On his return, therefore, from a Crusade, he proceeded straight to Peronne where he placed his own seal on the sepulchre. The figure of Fursa is now carried on the banner of the City of Peronne.

St. Fiacre of Meaux   c. 670
30 August

When public transport first made its appearance in Paris, it took the form of horse-drawn cabs which used as their terminus the Hotel St. Fiacre. Ever since, hired vehicles have been known in France as fiacres. An Irish saint, therefore, has the unusual distinction of being perpetuated in the French language. He has also the distinction of being the centre of one of the strongest cults in all France, a cult which had already started in his own lifetime, and there has also been a persistent tradition through the centuries that he was actually offered the Throne of Scotia, i.e. Ireland.

He appeared in the Diocese of Meaux about 626, and was given by the Bishop a hermitage at Breuil where he acquired extraordinary prestige for his sanctity, his concern for the poor and the suffering, and the remarkable cures which made his hermitage the talk of all France. The extent of his fame can be judged by the fact that the two later French saints regarded Fiacre as their special Patron. One was John of Matha, founder of the Trinitarians, who actually built himself a hermitage on what he called the ground hallowed by this Irishman. The other was St. Vincent de Paul.

38

Two of the most illustrious names in the history of the Church in France are strongly associated with the cult of St. Fiacre. One was Bossuet, the best known of all the Bishops of Meaux. The other was Cardinal Richelieu. Since these two had great influence with the French Royal Family, it is not surprising that royal pilgrims were frequently to be seen at the shrine of St. Fiacre. Indeed, Louis XI had already richly embellished the shrine and emblazoned on it the Royal Arms of France. Louis XIII and his Queen, Anne of Austria, invoked the saint's intercession to provide an heir, and both hailed the birth of Louis XIV as the answer to their prayer. Louis XIII is said to have been clasping in his hand a St. Fiacre medallion when he died.

Louis XIV and Louis XV both sought St. Fiacre's intercession to obtain a cure of the troublesome fistula, a painful ulcerous condition. Both were cured. St. Fiacre was credited with so many cures of this particular ailment that it has become known in France as "La maladie de St. Fiacre" – St. Fiacre's sickness". The remarkable connection between this saint and Royal personages includes even a King of England.

French sources record that Henry V, after the Battle of Agincourt, allowed his soldiers to vandalize the shrine of St. Fiacre at Meaux. According to an account of the incident, written by Denys Maslier, before the end of the same century, the cart which bore off the relics of the saint, stopped dead at the boundary of the monastery. The horses refused to move further and the project was abandoned. Popular tradition has made much of the fact that Henry V died on the Feast Day of Fiacre. It can well be imagined that this tradition lost none of its vitality when it became known that he died of haemorrhoids, a condition which the saint was reputed to cure regularly.

It is quite common for French towns and villages to be named after Irish saints. In the case of Fiacre, there are no less than three towns which bear his name, one in La Brie, another in Plougat and yet another in Brittany. There are 30 churches dedicated to him in France. An interesting custom connected with him still persists in Paris. This consists of gifts of flowers on his Feast Day to the Church of St. Ferdinand.

It is unusual for an Irish Saint who laboured outside Ireland to have created a strong cult in Ireland itself. In the case of Fiacre, pilgrimages were made for centuries to a shrine erected to his memory in Kilkenny. In Scotland, St. Fickers Bay, near Aberdeen, bears his name and a few miles away is the church of St. Fiacre.

St. Fiacre has the distinction of being the centre of study by a group of French scholars, known as the "Comité Nationale St. Fiacre". In 1970, they held an important Congress, partly in France, partly in Ireland, to mark the thirteenth centenary of his death. The proceedings of this Congress are contained in a publication on the life and influence of this famous saint, who is certainly one of the most carefully researched of all the Irish saints in Europe. This book has, moreover, done much to revive the memory of St. Fiacre in France, Luxembourg and Germany.

The publication which contains the proceedings of the Congress of 1970, held by the Comité Nationale St. Fiacre, sums up in one terse sentence its conclusion . . . "We are dealing, therefore, with a national celebrity". Such a judgement from French scholars is exceptional praise, and few indeed are those foreigners who have earned such a tribute from the French nation. St. Fiacre, the Irish monk who created the traditions of Meaux, has certainly earned a permanent place in the traditions of France.

Fiacre is the Patron of the gardeners of France. He died in 670 and his image has survived over the centuries as one of the great saints of that country. He is one of the most striking examples of those Irish Exiles for Christ who devoted their saintly life to the needy and the suffering in society. It was, in fact, the attention he paid to certain illnesses, normally ignored, which increasingly established his lasting prestige. He is traditionally held to have cured many syphilitics who, at that time, would have had difficulty in obtaining treatment, due to the attitudes towards this particular ailment. It is the compassion shown by Fiacre which more than anything else has created the enduring image of a true saint of the people.

St. Dymphna of Gheel (Belgium)   7th century
15 May

The story of St. Dymphna is unique among the accounts of Irish saints, and perhaps among the saints of the Church. Her cult is universal and she has the distinction of having built a tradition which has made the entire community of the town of Gheel in Belgium a refuge for the mentally afflicted and a world centre for the advanced study of mental health. Not the least remarkable feature of this story is that compassion or even tolerance for the mentally ill was not a feature of society until very recent times. Yet the example of Dymphna, thirteen centuries ago, was strong enough to conquer a universal neglect amounting often to hostility that was too often the fate of those afflicted in that way.

The story began, probably in the county Monaghan, where Dymphna's father was a pagan chieftain. His wife who, like Dymphna, was a Christian, died. Distracted by grief, he conceived the deranged idea that his daughter was the only woman who sufficiently resembled his wife to compensate for her loss. So he decided to marry her. Dymphna, horrified, fled with her chaplain, Gereborn, and two servants to Gheel where, in the few months left to her before her father tracked her down, she drew increasing attention for her devotion to the poor and the suffering. The result of her father's arrival was that all four were killed by the deranged chieftain. Not surprisingly, the whole story gripped the imagination of the entire countryside, especially as, according to tradition, cures of lunatics took place round her grave.

The Irish origins of Dymphna are entirely based on local tradition. There is no real evidence in Ireland to support her Irishness. However this is not uncommon with Irish saints on the continent. The reason for this is that their existence in Ireland did not call for any special record. Dymphna was not even a nun in a community. By contrast, when she arrived with three attendants in Gheel, her presence created interest. Her death and its attendant circumstances focused attention. Her country of origin would be part of the story, and there is no reason why Belgian tradition should firmly declare her Irish if she were not.

A strange development led to the relics of Gereborn being stolen, and he is now interred at Sonsbeck in Germany. There was at one time a curious body of thieves called "holy robbers" who specialised in removing sacred relics. In this case they failed to remove the relics of Dymphna, which have remained in St. Dymphna's Church in Gheel. It was centuries before a Bishop of Cambrai, faced with the growing veneration for Dymphna and the growth of interest in mental illness, arranged for her biography to be written, and it is this which has brought together the whole oral tradition. From that time, the veneration of Dymphna has steadily increased.

The name Dymphna has long been popular among Irish girls, and is increasingly so. This is not surprising since the interest in the care and treatment of mental illness in all its forms has become an important feature of modern society. It is not surprising either, since the cult of this Irish girl, whose personal experience and the resulting cult throughout the centuries, inspired the first and most lasting of the movements towards compassion and true understanding of those afflicted by mental illness, has steadily grown since then.

The feast day of Dymphna is observed in Ireland. Her festival is celebrated annually at Gheel. In America her cult is particularly strong and there is, in Ohio, a National Shrine to St. Dymphna, side by side with one of the most modern hospitals in the world. The Franciscan Mission Associates in America conduct a world-wide correspondence in her name, to fund their widespread activities for the poor and suffering, especially in Central America. Clearly the widespread and growing interest in mental illness which is evident in modern society, has given a new impetus to the cult of Dymphna who is regarded above all others as the Patroness of the mentally afflicted.

Kilian of Würzburg 689
8 July

A few years ago, in 1975, the German community in Ireland opened the German High School in Dublin and dedicated it to St. Kilian. This delicate compliment to the Irish people, symbolised the long history of Irish missionary activity in Germany, and is typical of the generous acknowledgement of the debt Germany owes to a long succession of Irish missioners in that country.

High among these is Kilian of Würzburg from Co. Cavan in Ireland. About 680 he arrived in Würzburg with two Irish companions, Colman and Totnan (also called Tadhg). They obtained many converts and established their fame far and wide. Among the converts was Duke Gospert himself, the Lord of the territory.

Kilian and his companions were typical of all Irish missioners in one important respect. They spoke up fearlessly against any breach of faith or morals. In this case they openly rebuked the Duke for his irregular marriage, which, since his wife was the widow of his brother, was contrary to the laws of the Church. She planned and had carried out the assassination of all three Irishmen.

The immediate effect of this martyrdom was to initiate a strong cult which rapidly took hold in Germany and has made the name of Kilian an object of veneration as far away as Vienna. To this day, the feast day of the three saints, the Kilianfest, is one of the better-known festivals of the German people, a custom incidentally also carried out by Germans in the U.S.A., and by expatriate Germans all over the world.

The strength of this cult came to the ears of Pope Zachary, who, in 752, permitted public veneration of the three martyrs. It was almost normal from the time of Charlemagne onwards for Emperors to make a pilgrimage to the shrine at Würzburg. Boniface, the Anglo-Saxon Apostle of Germany, created Würzburg a bishopric in honour of Kilian.

The names of illustrious Irishmen who visited the city at one time or another, indicate that it was regarded over the centuries as of special Irish interest. As late as 1134, an Irish monastery, one of the group of twelve belonging to Ratisbon was set up in Würzburg, and in 1650 a famous Irish historian, Father Stephen White, S. J., chose it as the centre of his studies of Irish antiquities in Germany. Kilian's Bible is exposed on his feast day on the High Altar of the Cathedral Church there.

St. Colman of Melk, Austria   1012
13 October

The imposing Abbey of Melk, on the Danube in Austria, has a very definite Celtic tradition, for it contains the Shrine of Saint Colman, who was martyred near Melk in 1012, and it is the object of pilgrimages and veneration throughout Austria, Bavaria and Hungary.

The name Colman occurs more often than any other among the saints of Ireland. One Irish historian estimates that there are no less than 300 Colmans listed in the various martyrologies. St. Colman of Melk is probably the most universal of all those who bear the name. The account of his martyrdom and the strength and extent of his cult, provide material for one of the most absorbing stories of Irish sanctity.

The Emperor, Henry V, was intrigued by the devotion throughout his territory, to Koloman, the name commonly used there for Colman. He ordered an investigation into the history of the cult. A similar enquiry ordered by Pope Paschal II led him to grant an indulgence to pilgrims at Colman's Shrine. In later times three more Popes, Clement VI, Innocent VI and Leo X also granted indulgencies.

The enquiries revealed the fact that Colman was a pilgrim from Ireland to the Holy Land. He arrived in Stockerau in Austria at an unfortunate time. Armed conflict was going on against the Bohemians and Colman was arrested as a spy. His ignorance of the language added to the suspicion and he was tortured and hanged.

Traditions of sanctity grew up immediately, added to by unusual features of his death. He was hanged, as Jesus was crucified, between two thieves. The bodies were left hanging. Wild beasts and birds of prey tore to pieces the bodies of the two thieves. The body of Colman was still untouched after nearly two years. The scaffolding which formed his gallows had sent forth branches and had flowered.

Such are the traditions which have led to the cult of St. Colman of Melk. The Emperor erected an elaborate shrine for his remains at Melk and they were transferred to the Abbey where they have lain ever since. The presence of these remains has ensured a constant stream of pilgrims to the Abbey for more than 800 years.

It is worth recalling that many traditional saints have been accepted in other ways than by canonisation. For an important effect of canonisation is to make universal what is otherwise merely local. In the case of Colman, four Popes granted indulgences to pilgrims at his tomb. As he stands at the pinnacle of the Catholic Church, an official declaration of this kind from a Pope carries with it the stamp of universality. At the time, the other universal power was the Emperor. His interest in Colman had also its effect in making his veneration universal. He was not the only Irish saint whose memory has been endorsed by a Pope. Nor was he the only one to be so endorsed by an Emperor, but he may have been the only one to have been endorsed by both of the universal powers.

Obviously, the story of Colman contains unique features, which have combined to create a strong cult from the beginning. To add to these, there is no evidence that he was a missionary or even a priest. He was a lone pilgrim. Again, like so many other Irish exiles or even travellers of the time, the facts concerning him, including his Irish origins, have come, not from Ireland, but from those among whom he was martyred and by whom he is venerated.

Marianus Scotus of Ratisbon   1088
9 February

Muiredach MacRobartaigh (MacGroarty) was one of a noble Donegal family kinsman of the O'Donnels, who were the hereditary keepers of the Cathach, or Battle Book of Colmcille. In the year 1067 he left for Rome, which he never reached. A temporary stop in Germany led to his becoming a scribe at Ratisbon, and the founder of an Irish abbey, out of which ultimately arose twelve Irish abbeys in Europe.

He stayed by chance in a pilgrim's hostel, maintained by nuns under the Abbess Emma. When she discovered his extraordinary skills in turning out manuscripts she persuaded him to attach himself to St. Peter's Church in Ratisbon where he produced manuscripts which have become literary treasures. The most famous of these are the Epistles of St. Paul, now held in the Imperial Library in Vienna. The astonishing quality and volume of his writings brought him a reputation for sanctity, based on the popular belief that he was filled with the Holy Spirit.

In 1076 he was given charge of the Church of St. Peter, and there he built his Abbey of St. Peter. His fame had spread to Ireland and so many monks arrived from there that within ten years plans were already made for the foundation of another Irish Abbey. Marianus himself died in 1088, but his prestige continued for decades afterwards during which the traffic of monks from Ireland never ceased.

In the year of his death, the greatest of these Abbeys, St. James, was set up, also at Ratisbon. The Irish traditions of these Abbeys are illustrated by the fact that St. James, and others which followed, were assisted at their foundation by funds sent from Ireland. The Irish character of these communities, and the privileges which were granted to them, were confirmed by a series of Popes, Callixtus, Innocent II, and Eugenius III. Within one hundred years after the original foundation of St. Peter's, there were twelve Abbeys in all, and the Abbot of St. James', the Mother House, was granted by the Emperor the privilege of the Half-Eagle on his Coat of Arms, the right to the title of Prince, and the status of independent Statehood for the entire Congregation of Abbeys. The other Abbeys which arose from the two at Ratisbon were: Würzburg, Nuremberg, Constance, St. Mary's and St. George's in Vienna, Memmingen, Erfurt, Kelheim, Oels and Schottenburg in Silesia.

The establishment of these Abbeys, six centuries after the death of St. Patrick, is specially significant in Irish history. It has often been said that the Viking raids on Ireland put a stop to the work of the Schools of Ireland and, in fact, closed the Golden Age. Yet the group of Abbeys launched by Marianus, were not initiated until sixty years after the Battle of Clontarf which ended the Viking episode for ever.

The existence of these Abbeys, closely associated with Irish monks and Irish traditions, entered into a period of dispute which had become inevitable for a curious reason. The ancient name "Scot", used since Roman times for the Irishman was still so used in Germany, and indeed Marianus himself was described as Scotus. In Scotland itself, a national monarchy had existed for some two centuries, and the name Scotland or Scotia had become increasingly used solely for that country.

In 1515, as a result of great pressure from monks in Scotland Pope Leo X admitted Scottish monks into possession of St. James at Ratisbon, and the Abbeys at Constance or Erfurt. At that time Scotland was an independent kingdom, unlike Ireland. Whatever the arguments used, there can be no doubt that these Abbeys were not only Irish foundations, but were founded more than once with funds from Ireland, and staffed by Irish monks. German scholars have many times recorded all this, and apparently Popes who lived at the time accepted them as Irish. Leo X, who ruled in favour of Scottish, rather than Irish origins, lived four and a half centuries after Marianus founded St. Peter's. Numerous lists of saints invariably acknowledge his Irish origins and normally also his Irish name. It is also something of a mystery why the Pope who awarded three Abbeys to Scottish monks, did not apply the same ruling to nine others.

This group of abbeys is known in Germany as the Schottenklöster. *The Dictionary of Scottish History* states under this heading that the abbeys were Irish foundations, and specifically mentions Ratisbon, Constance and Erfurt, the three abbeys granted by Pope Leo XIII to the Scottish claimants. The Dictionary of Scottish History was published in Scotland in 1977 and the authors were Gordon Donaldson and Robert S. Morpeth.

Gall of St. Gall, Switzerland   c. 640
16 October

In 612 an Irish monk, "an exile for Christ", set up a rude cross in Switzerland, to mark the site of his oratory and cell. More than thirteen centuries later this spot is the revered site of one of the truly great Abbeys of Europe, and of the Swiss city and Canton of St. Gallen. Gall himself, was a companion of Columbanus and parted from him as the latter made his way over the Alps to found the other great Abbey at Bobbio.

The prestige of Gall was such that he was beseeched many times to accept the highest honours, including at least one bishopric, at Constance. He preferred to pursue his destiny at St. Gall, and his presence there ensured that for some centuries his Abbey was to be a centre of Irish missionaries. One distinguished historian estimates that Gall was venerated in some sixty centres in Switzerland and a dozen in Germany. Another historian notes the fact that when Francis of Assisi, in 1211, first assembled his followers it was in the church of St. Gall in Florence. In the city of St Gall there is a great cathedral in his name.

In the 9th century perhaps the most famous scholar and teacher in Europe was the Irishman, Moengal, who raised the status of the Abbey even higher. The great Tutilo, the father of musical teaching, was one of his students, generally identified as the Irish Tuathal. Indeed the Abbey was foremost in providing manuscripts of Gregorian chant throughout the Middle Ages.

Gall's monastery lasted till its suppression in 1805 during Napoleon's resettlement of the Helvetic Republic (Switzerland). It really began its illustrious career about a century after the death of Gall, in 645. For all the succeeding centuries it was recognised as a leading centre of ecclesiastical and lay scholarship, and the Library is the repository of one of the greatest treasures of Irish manuscripts anywhere in the world. Among other priceless possessions is the first Latin–German dictionary in existence, prepared and completed by an Irish monk in the eighth century.

Gall was credited with miracles from the start of his mission in St. Gall. In the first few days, a bear came out of the woods, to be ordered by Gall in the name of Jesus Christ, to return and bring wood for his fire. Needless to say, the order was obeyed and forms the basis of the tradition of his sanctity. Veneration grew rapidly as he proceeded with his pastoral work, and his intercession was constantly sought. A popular legend concerns his cure of the epileptic daughter of a local Duke.

He died about the year 640, and his hermitage became the centre of pilgrimages. His relics were considered to be so holy that more than once his tomb was plundered by "holy robbers". In 720, the King Charles Martel appointed a certain Othmar to set up the Abbey in perpetuity, and to safeguard the relics of Gall. This was taken to be the first real founding of the great Abbey, which arose out of the veneration inspired by Gall.

Fridolin of Sackingen, Switzerland   6th century
6 March

There has over the centuries been widespread devotion to Fridolin in Bavaria, Austria and Switzerland. He seems to have started his missionary work in Poitiers in France, where he performed a notable service in collecting the relics of St. Hilary and restoring the church. In fact he had a special devotion for this saint and later set up monasteries in his name, including his most famous one at Sackingen on the Rhine. Another was at Chur, also in Switzerland. This Abbey had a special Irish tradition and sculptured stones of Irish design are still to be seen there.

Fridolin is one of those whose Irishness has been in dispute. It would seem that he was not specially recorded in Ireland. On the other hand he has been accepted as Irish from the time of his arrival, although the earliest "Life" of him, written by a monk of Sackingen, was not written till five centuries after Fridolin's death. However, this author claimed to base his facts on a much earlier biography. A still later account of Fridolin, written by Peter Canis, usually known as Canisius the Jesuit who led the Counter-Reformation in Germany, states positively that Fridolin was Irish.

In this connection, it is worth recording that Fridolin seems to be one of the few Irish Saints whose nationality is specially stressed on the Feast Day. In Sackingen, on 6 March, the houses are decorated with the flags of Germany, Switzerland and Ireland.

Cathaluds (Cathal) of Taranto, Italy 7th century
10 May

Cathal, or Cathaldus (the Latin) or Cataldo, as he is known to Italians, was Bishop of Taranto, and is one of the most popular of all saints in Italy. His name is used on churches and building all over Italy, in Malta, and even into France, especially in areas of Italian influence. He has the distinction of being the subject of a painting on a pillar in the Basilica of the Nativity in Bethlehem.

His Irish identity was discovered only two or three centuries after his death when his relics were being recovered during the rebuilding of the Cathedral of Taranto. A small golden cross, of Irish workmanship, was with the relics, and subsequent researchers identified him with Cathal, a teacher at Lismore. The Office on his Feast Day makes several references to his Irish origin.

-The widespread veneration of Cataldo became a national cult, especially strong in Southern Italy, at the time of the transfer of his relics on his Feast Day in 1017. Four remarkable cures took place as the relics were being taken to their resting place in the new Cathedral and he has become very strongly venerated as the Patron of Southern Italy. There is a town called San Cataldo in Sicily and another on the South East coast of Italy. The name Cataldo is a popular name for Italian boys.

Donato (Donagh) of Fiesole, Italy 876
22 October

Tradition has it that Donato and his Irish companion, Andrew, who became his deacon, were passing through Fiesole in 829, and Donato was invited to assume the vacant bishopric. Fiesole, known as the Mother of Florence, was a very important city. At that time, the faithful longed for a strong bishop who would protect the Faith, if necessary as a military leader, a role often assumed by the bishops in those times. In addition, the King, Lothair, was specially interested in Donato's scholarship and hoped he might build up the schools of Fiesole. For forty-seven years, he conducted an active and fruitful apostolate. More than once he led expeditions against the Saracens and before he died he had obtained from the King a Charter of Independence for the bishops of Fiesole, with power to impose taxes and administer their own laws.

He had a special devotion to Brigid of Kildare, and he completed St. Brigid's Church at Piacenza in 850, placing it under the care and authority of Columban's great Abbey at Bobbio. This Church was declared a national monument in Italy in 1911. His name Donato, sometimes in the form of Dino or Dona, is common among Italian boys, and is also the origin of the German name Donat. He wrote quite considerably, notably two separate lives of St. Brigid, one in prose and one in verse. In his time, Fiesole was a noted centre for Irish pilgrims going to Rome, and he was a powerful influence in building and preserving the Irish character of Bobbioo.

Brendan of Clonfert (The Navigator) 486–578
16 May

There is a widespread impression that the unusual history of Saint Brendan is divided into two distinct parts. The one best known is the history of his famous voyages, the other is his achievements as a monk labouring for Christ in the early days of Christianity in Ireland.

It is always necessary in any biographical account of this exceptional Irishman to clarify where these two roles came together and, in view of the interest caused by his voyages, to put into perspective the importance of his contribution to the Christian mission.

If he had never left Ireland, he would have merited a distinguished place among the traditional saints of Ireland for what he achieved there. He was the founder of at least two well-known establishments, Ardfert in Kerry and Clonfert in Galway. Perhaps the greatest testimony to the enduring cult which he created is the fact that the Bishopric associated with Clonfert has survived for more than fourteen centuries as one of the very oldest, continuous Sees in Ireland. The *Annuario Pontificio,* the Pontifical Year Book, lists the Bishopric of Clonfert as being founded in 550.

Dedications to Saint Brendan in Ireland are very numerous. Among the better known are Mount Brandon in Kerry and at least three Holy Wells in his name, two in Mayo and one in Kerry. He is almost as well-known in Scotland. Even in the Faroe Isles, there is a creek which still bears the name Brandarsvik, Brendan's Creek.

Any idea that his seafaring and his missionary activities were entirely separate is an incorrect judgement. Brendan saw himself as extending God's Kingdom on earth. He went out to find other souls for God. In this task, he is said to have evangelised in Scotland and to have opened up Iceland and the Faroes for other Irish missioners to develop. His primary dedication to missionary work is well illustrated by the legends and, indeed, written accounts of how he even imposed religious rules on board his boats. The story of his celebrating Mass on the back of a whale is one of the standard legends in the saga of Saint Brendan.

It is, undoubtedly, however, the wider history of his voyages which projected him into history as one of the earliest and most interesting pioneers in exploration of new lands. Some centuries after his death, an unknown scholar, possibly Irish, put together the oral legends and launched into universal fame the Navigatio Brendani, the Voyage of Brendan. This work was read increasingly by medieval scholars, was translated into all the main languages and became a text book in the schools of Europe.

The visionary land which Saint Brendan seemed to have in mind bore a close resemblance to a legendary land in the mythology of the Gaelic race. It bore various names and various descriptions. Two of the most persistent in the Gaelic tradition were the Tir na n'Og, the land of the young, and Hy-Brasil, the Island of The Blest. As Saint Brendan, who belonged to a famous Irish royal family, was an early Christian in Ireland, it is very probable that he had in mind a Gaelic tradition which he visualised in a Christian context.

The tradition has been that, in fact, what he was seeking in his major voyage, was the continent of America and so the legend has persisted that he actually found it. It has been said that Christopher Columbus, who studied at Pavia University which grew out of schools set up by the Irish scholars, read the Navigatio Brendani there and may have developed from that the ambitious idea which finally led to the final discovery of America.

Historians have stated that Columbus visited Clonfert while planning his voyage. Mary Ryan D'Arcy, quoting Professor G. A. Little, the author of *Brendan the Navigator,* states that official

Spanish archives contain the names of Irishmen who accompanied Columbus on his voyage. *The Story of the Irish Race,* edited by Seumas McManus, contains the information that an early biographer of Columbus, a Father Tornitore, states that the first man ashore in the New World was the Irish gentleman farmer from Clonfert, Patrick McGuire.

Those who maintain that accounts like the Navigatio Brendani contain too much fantasy to be taken seriously, must consider that at least twice serious exploring scholars of modern times have stripped the fantasy from the facts, and carried out successful voyages as a result. One was William Verity, of Fort Lauderdale, Florida who, in 1966, made a solo voyage from Florida to Ireland, returning in the same way in 1969. His purpose, as he said, was "to put the Brendan legend in working order".

In 1977, the Oxford research scholar, Tim Severin, carried out a voyage from Ireland to Newfoundland, using the same type of craft and following the same route as Brendan. In the book he published after his voyage, Severin described how he had been able to see, beneath the highly imaginative descriptions and fantasy pervading the Navigatio Brendanii, a clear scientific basis. In his conclusion, he made it clear that Brendan's voyage had been proved to be possible, although it was not proved that Brendan had actually achieved it.

It is not surprising that commentators through the ages have found it difficult to find a clear link between what seem to be two outstanding careers carved out within one lifetime. The fact is that Saint Brendan was guided by spiritual motives. This was clear in his work in Ireland. His famous voyages were, to him, the means of bringing the message of Christ to those who could not otherwise receive it.

In the event, he became one of the most discussed of all the illustrious company of Irish saints. His prominence has never faded. Even now inscriptions, allegedly in the ogham script of Irish Gaelic, which have been found in Newfoundland and on the North-East coast of the USA, are being studied on the general assumption that they bear out the Brendan legend. Even in the most unlikely places, his name has penetrated. Some scholar of the future may find it an interesting field of research to trace the origin of the widespread tradition among the Spanish people of Central America, which goes under the name of "El Caballo Blanco de San Brendano", the White Horse of Saint Brendan.

CHAPTER IV

Papal Recognition of Irish Saints

It would be a truism to say that canonisation is the supreme honour which the Church can award to a Servant of God. To Irish people, as to many others, this process always raises questions as to the status of popular saints who are honoured entirely by tradition, and have not been canonised.

It cannot be repeated too often that the Holy See has the greatest respect for this kind of tradition and indeed seems to regard it very often as being sufficiently valid not to require any further endorsement at the highest level in the Church. Irish people, who wonder what is the distinction between the two classes of saints, should bear in mind that, on balance, the greatest figures in the history of Christianity are uncanonised saints. Patrick, Brigid, Colmcille and a vast number of Irish saints were not canonised, but then neither were St. Peter, Paul, Augustine nor a long line of others.

It would, in this context, be wrong to assume that the Holy See decided not to enter officially into the recognition of popular saints by canonisation. On examination, it can safely be said that Popes in the past have explicitly endorsed the sanctity of Irish popular saints in a number of ways. One was by the granting of Indulgences to pilgrims at the shrines of such saints. Another was by authorising Masses to a saint on the feast day. Yet a third consisted in accepting the title of Saint in approving devotions or even religious Orders dedicated to one saint or another.

The most obvious examples of this last process, officially listed in the *Annuario Pontificio*, or Vatican Yearbook, are the St. Patrick's Fathers and Brothers, the Fathers and Sisters of St. Columbanus and the Sisters of St. Brigid. Indeed, the Pope's Secretary currently is a member of the Order of the St. Patrick's Fathers. Churches in the name of Irish Saints are common, the most significant in this whole connection being St. Patrick's

Church in Rome itself, known also as the Irish National Church and the Titular Church of the present Primate of All Ireland, Cardinal O'Fiaich, Archbishop of Armagh.

To attempt to document, throughout the ages, every case when a Pope has given a positive endorsement to the veneration of a traditional Irish saint, would be an impossible task. Here it is intended merely to illustrate the interest of the Holy See in Irish sanctity by listing the canonised saints of Ireland and some of those whose sanctity has been acknowledged by specific action by particular Popes.

Because the Pope stands at the pinnacle of the Roman Catholic Church, the direct intervention of the Holy See in the question of the sanctity of an Irish saint, whether by full canonisation or by official acts of a particular Pope, endows a new universality to that which may already have been imparted by tradition. Those names which now follow are clear examples of this process of universality.

In reading these names, it should be noted that two Irish saints described in the chapter on the Golden Age of Ireland, are examples of Papal approval. One was Kilian of Würzburg whose public veneration, with that of his two companions, Colman and Tadhg (Totnan) was approved by Pope Zachary. The other was Colman of Melk, in whose case four different Popes granted Indulgences to pilgrims at his shrine.

In 1975, Pope Paul VI solemnly canonised the Irish Archbishop, Oliver Plunkett, who thus became the fifth canonised Irish Saint. The event was, of course, widely publicised in Ireland and almost all the comments in the National Press added the information that this was the first canonisation of an Irish saint since Laurence O'Toole, canonised in 1225. In fact, almost the entire Irish nation overlooked the fact that Fearghal (or Virgilius), an Irish Archbishop of Salzburg, Austria was canonised in 1233.

Ireland is a country whose saints are something of a phenomenon in the history of the Church. To be sure, the best known are popular or traditional saints whose Golden Age had come to an end, before the present system of canonisation reserved to the Holy See had begun. Since the system has so far produced only five canonised Irish saints, the virtual indifference to the status of Sillao of Lucca and Fearghal of Salzburg, among their own people, seems to call for some explanation of Irish attitudes in the important matter of Irish saints.

On the face of it, the indications are that the Irish people are less interested in canonised saints than in those created by the spontaneous veneration of the Irish of the past. This sort of tradition is in no way unique to Ireland. What is unique to Ireland, perhaps, is the purely fortuitous fact that the abrupt change in the whole course of Irish history which began eight centuries ago when the first Norman invaders arrived has had an historic effect on certain national attitudes.

Irish history since 1169 has been dominated by the question of Irish nationhood. The position on this issue of the one great national institution which spans the period before and after this historic event, the Church, has necessarily loomed large in the thinking of the people. The Irish people have sought to make a distinction between their political and their spiritual needs, and over the centuries, they have shown a tendency to reinforce their great saints of the early centuries rather to the detriment of those who followed, and that means, in particular, the canonised saints.

The events connected with the Norman invasion has made nationhood a permanent feature of Irish history ever since. In that situation, it is perhaps understandable that Irish saints who laboured outside Ireland, and whose prestige is principally sustained by non-Irish devotees, are less in the minds of the Irish at home. This is a principal reason for the apparent lack of interest in Virgilius of Salzburg. It is also a curious fact, not without significance, that all five canonised saints died outside Ireland, and the bodies of all of them lie outside Ireland.

It is timely to suggest that there is a stark contrast arising from this in the fact that several times the bodies of national heroes have been brought back to Ireland for burial ,and to provide an occasion for a national gesture. The Irish people have never mounted a national demand for the remains of their official saints.

The evidence, therefore, seems to indicate that saints are accepted, with due pride, only as part of Ireland's great religious history. It also indicates that they do not, in the main, fall into the category of national heroes. If this is a correct judgement of the Irish attitude then the Irish people have not made a fair evaluation of the five saintly Irishmen under review in this study. For all of them were deeply involved in problems concerned with the conditions in Ireland in their time. Even Fearghal, written off as he appears to be by his people, faced serious problems relating to his status as an Irish monk, even in far away Austria.

A main purpose of this study is to adjust the record in regard to these great Irishmen. The honours of the altar, as represented by their canonisation, are conclusive evidence of their sanctity. It remains, however, to bring home to their people that Ireland owes them an honoured place in the history of the nation. All of them had, throughout their illustrious career, some aspect of Irish interest firmly in their minds as they pursued their way to the honours of the altar.

It was said above that canonisation is conclusive evidence of their sanctity. It should be added that there is probably no research enquiry, which this process is, which can compare with a Papal enquiry in its thorough, painstaking techniques, nor in the resources for research at its disposal. It can be assumed, with the maximum certainty, that the doubts, rumours, calumnies and falsehoods with which these Irish saints had to cope to an extent were fully and finally disposed of by the process leading to canonisation which, it can be said, was their complete vindication before the bar of history.

In the brief notes, therefore, which are the subject of this booklet, the contributions of each of these five saints to Irish history are stressed. There can be little doubt that the Irish people, devoted as they undoubtedly are to their Faith, have accorded less honour to their canonised saints than their record merits. It is hoped that the brief notes on each of them will help to bring about new attitudes affecting their image among their own people.

Sillaeus (Sillao, Siollan) of Lucca, Italy   1100
May 21

In the year 1183, Pope Lucius III authorised the cult of the Irish Bishop, Siollan, known in the Archdiocese of Lucca, as Sillao. By this public declaration, the Pope, in fact, canonised St. Sillao. In view of the truly unusual circumstances surrounding the association of this saint with Lucca, it should be stressed that this Pope was himself a native of Lucca, completely familiar with the whole tradition of Sillao, which included the fact that he was an Irish Bishop.

Three years before the canonisation, that is in 1180, the nuns of St. Giustina in Lucca, who had been disturbed by the cessation of miracles which previously had been a remarkable feature of this shrine, and the consequent fall in the devotion which had formerly been accorded to St. Sillao decided to open the coffin. When they did so, they found a Latin inscription identifying the body as that of the saint and containing the following phrase: ". . . qui in Hibernia episcopus fuit . . ." thus opening up for the first time the remarkable story of the Irish Bishop who died in Lucca.

Eminent Italian scholars have conducted detailed research into the story of St. Sillao, and their combined conclusions are quite positive, and place the story of his life in the eleventh century. They have no doubt that he was a monk in an Abbey of St. Brendan, possibly Clonfert, of which he became Abbot. He was subsequently made a Bishop, although it is not clear to which diocese he was appointed. It is possible that it was the Diocese of Clonfert.

Sillao was not satisfied until he saw the Pope that his consecration was fully valid, and he went to Rome to be consecrated by Pope Gregory VII. On his return to Ireland, his sister Mionghar, known to Italians as Hermengarda, decided also to make a pilgrimage to Rome. She stopped on the way at Lucca, where she was subjected to a tempestuous wooing by an Italian nobleman, Suffred, a widower. After nine years of marriage to him, she retired to the Convent of St. Giustina, where she died.

Quite fortuitously, St. Sillao arrived at that time in Lucca, on a second visit to Rome to report to the Pope on certain serious problems which faced him in his diocese. On his way back, he arrived again in Lucca and died almost immediately in 1100 in the Convent of St. Giustina where his sister had died shortly before.

The immediate sequel to his death was the most remarkable part of the story. Miracles were so commonly reported that a strong devotion to the saint grew immediately. So did the contributions from rich devotees. The nuns of St. Giustina were presented with a demand from Suffred, trading on his relationship with the saint, to be given a third share of this income. The nuns, well aware that this was a shameless request, were at the same time intimidated by the fact that this nobleman was probably the most powerful influence in Lucca and capable of causing great harm to the whole convent. With the greatest misgivings, they agreed to his conditions.

The miracles immediately ceased. The nuns watched with dismay the rapid decline in the devotion which had been proving a major influence in the growth of their convent, and indeed it was faced with extinction eighty years after the death of the saint. It was at this point that the nuns decided to investigate the tomb of Sillao, hoping to find some clue to the withdrawal of the saint's favours. It was then that the inscription was found, which was referred to above, declaring St. Sillao to be an Irish bishop.

What was more important was that the current head of Suffred's family, being made aware of the bargain made by Suffred, immediately denounced his conduct and refused to have anything to do with it. This renunciation was followed by a resumption of the miracles, the first since Suffred made his infamous demands. Tree years later, in 1183, Pope Lucius III canonised St. Sillao.

This decision by the Pope must be regarded as powerful proof of the essentials of the story of St. Sillao. Papal investigations leading to a canonisation are a very complete research process, and leave no scope for any improbabilities. In addition, this Pope was very familiar with the history of Lucca, his native town, and would certainly have considered very carefully all the circumstances of St. Sillao's presence in Lucca. From an Irish point of view, he must have been aware of the documentary evidence of the saint's Irish origins and his status as bishop, which he apparently endorsed.

Serious scholars in Ireland hesitate to claim St. Sillao as an Irish saint since his Irish origins are obscure. It is not uncommon, however, for saints to be venerated outside Ireland as Irish saints, while proof of their Irish origins are not available in Ireland. In the case of St. Sillao, it should be borne in mind that the Italian scholars who accept the fact that he was an Irish bishop, include the Pope who canonised him. There seems to be no reason to doubt the fact that St. Sillao belongs to the company of Irish saints. Not only is this the case, but it opens up an interesting situation. For, if St. Sillao was indeed Irish, then he belongs to the small select group of canonised Irish saints. He is, in fact, the first of them, since he was canonised in 1183, seven years before St. Malachy, generally considered in Ireland to be the first Irishman to be canonised.

St. Malachy of Armagh   1094–1148
4 November

When Pope Eugenius III became Supreme Pontiff in 1145, he had to go into exile for the first two years of his pontificate to escape the sustained hostility of the people of Rome. The Pope, who was a Cistercian, sought advice and comfort from the most famous of all Cistercians, St. Bernard of Clairvaux. The advice the Pope got was to model his life and conduct on the Irishman, Malachy. In later years, this same Pope was to make on Ireland's behalf the most momentous decision in the whole history of the Irish Church. For it was Eugenius III who set up the Archbishops of Ireland, and ensured for ever the independence of the Church in Ireland, and this he did because of his reverence for Malachy who made the request on behalf of his own people.

Malachy was born in 1094. During his lifetime, the whole future

of the Church in Ireland was the subject of repeated petitions to
Rome from the Bishops of England, to have the Church in Ireland
placed under the authority of Canterbury. The reason for this
was a number of alleged abuses, the most serious being that important Church institutions had become hereditary in certain
families, who not only appointed Abbots from laymen in their
families but appropriated the property and income. How serious
this had become may be judged from the fact that Malachy's own
uncle, the brother of his mother, held the Abbacy of Bangor in
lay succession. More serious still was that Armagh, the See of
Patrick, was also held in lay succession by another family.

It was fortunate for Ireland that the Primate at Armagh at the
time was Ceallach, himself a layman, who wanted to end what
he could see was a scandalous situation. He took Holy Orders to
set right that part of the problem. His next step was to ensure that
the succession should continue and perpetuate proper ecclesiastical control of Bishoprics and Abbeys, and he very quickly
chose Malachy as his eventual successor. He ordained him when
he was 25 and sent him for training to Malchus of Waterford who
was a leader of the growing movement to get rid of the whole
problem of lay control of Church establishments.

By the time Malachy returned, he was completely aware of the
urgency of this reform. It was now widely felt that the Holy See
might at any time decide to make the Church in Ireland a part of
the English Church. Malachy shared the view that, unless Irishmen carried out these reforms in Ireland, it would become the
responsibility of others. From that time on, Malachy's name became more and more associated with successful reform. His reputation for sanctity, amounting to veneration in his own lifetime,
was of enormous help not only throughout Ireland but in Rome.

It was not by chance that Ceallach, whose ultimate goal was to
reform the See of Armagh, sent Malachy to put things right at
Bangor, where Malachy's own uncle was in possession. In a re-
markably short space of time, his uncle not only resigned all his
hereditary rights, but became a monk. From there, Malachy went
to Iveragh in County Kerry where he founded a monastery,
hoping thus to be allowed to fulfil the ambition he carried with
him all his life to become a monk, an ambition which circumstances combined to deny him. Later, he was refused permission
by the Pope to enter the monastery of Clairvaux, under St.
Bernard, since the Pope decided that his work for the Irish
Church must continue.

In 1125, Ceallach persuaded him to become Bishop of Down

and Connor, which Malachy accepted with great reluctance. In 1129, Ceallach died, having named Malachy as his successor at Armagh. Simultaneously, a lay kinsman of Ceallach took possession. Had Malachy wished, he could have summoned overwhelming support to force the claimant out, but he preferred to avoid violence and to claim only the spiritual primacy. The death of the lay claimant was followed by the succession of another, but this time, in spite of Malachy's distaste for force, the reforming party made it clear that the lay claimant must abdicate all his rights which he promptly did. So, in 1137, Malachy who felt that his object had now been achieved resigned the Primacy to Gelasius, and set out for Rome.

It was during this journey that he first met St. Bernard of Clairvaux who was establishing his great reputation as the reformer of the Cistercians. This was the sort of activity which most appealed to Malachy and he decided to enter the community. Unfortunately for him, Pope Innocent II refused permission and, instead, made him Papal Legate in Ireland. At the same time, the Pope accepted from him petitions for the establishment of Archbishops in Armagh and Cashel. In terms of Irish history, this was the crowning achievement of Malachy's life, for his saintly image and his high reputation in Rome was to lead, four years after his death in 1148, to what many consider to be the greatest event in the history of the Church in Ireland.

In 1152, Pope Eugenius III probably on the advice of Bernard of Clairvaux, finally acted on the promise made by Pope Innocent II to grant the pallium, the symbol of the Archbishop, to Armagh and Cashel. Instead, however, of granting two, he added Dublin and Tuam. This gesture took everybody by surprise, mingled with joy and relief in Ireland. In England, by contrast, it was regarded as something of a rebuff, a clear indication that the Holy See had finally decided to establish and maintain the independence of the Church in Ireland. Moreover, the Holy See had placed the Archbishops strictly in accordance with the ancient history of Ireland, one in each of the kingdoms of Ulster, Leinster, Munster and Connaught.

It was during Malachy's journey to Rome that he is said to have performed a miracle in Scotland. It seems that the son of King David was on the point of death when Malachy prayed for his recovery, which was immediate. It was also during this journey that he delivered to Pope Innocent II the prophecies about the Popes, for which Malachy's name is most widely known. It is also said that Malachy was the originator of one of the most famous prophecies in Ireland, according to which there will be the Peace of Christ over all Ireland when the Palm and the Shamrock meet. This is taken to mean when St. Patrick's Day occurs on Palm Sunday. This prophecy was already referred to in the notes on Saint Patrick (see p. 19).

Malachy set out again for Rome in 1148 to report as Papal Legate to Pope Eugenius III and to press for the Archbishops promised by Innocent II. It happened, however, that when Malachy reached Clairvaux, he found that the Pope had just left, after the visit during which Bernard had recommended Malachy as a model for the Pope to follow. God had willed that they were not to meet. Malachy died at Clairvaux. He was the immediate object of veneration from the entire community. Bernard, in the requiem which he conducted for Malachy, boldly used the prayer for a confessor bishop, in the certainty that Malachy had gone straight into Heaven. In effect, Bernard assumed from the moment of his death that the Church would canonise Malachy.

Bernard was the biographer of Malachy. In the biography, he stressed the extent of Malachy's sanctity and how providential for Ireland that was at that time. The respect and veneration which Bernard had for Malachy played its part in his canonisation. For it was from the monks of Clairvaux led by Bernard that the impetus came for Malachy's canonisation in 1190. It is worth noting that his was one of the very early official canonisations. Indeed, the period which elapsed between his death and his elevation to the honours of the altar was quite a short one, less than half a century.

Malachy deserves an honoured place in the history of the Irish people. His part in bringing about the permanent independence of the Irish Church is beyond dispute, and no Irishman should underestimate the importance of that event. Had the situation developed as it appeared to be developing at the time, the Irish Church might well have passed for ever under the control of Canterbury. As it is, the independence of the Irish Church is so complete that it has even survived the political upheavals which began shortly after the death of Malachy. Even the political division of Ireland, represented by partition, has not affected the Church, for the Primacy still remains in the north, maintaining undisputed authority over all Ireland.

It is doubtful whether Malachy foresaw all this, as all the implications of English interest in Ireland did not become clear for twenty years after his death. His immediate interest was to reform the Church in Ireland and to secure its independence. That was his destiny and his greatest memorial in the history of Ireland. The destiny he had wished for himself was denied him. He was never allowed to enter a monastery and dedicate himself to that life.

Whether or nor Malachy was the author of the famous prophecies attributed to him, they have had the effect of placing him in a position which is unique not only among the saints in Ireland, but of all the saints in the Church. For every time a new Pope assumes the Chair of Peter, Malachy's prophecies are always recalled in the world press, amid speculation as to the significance of his predictions in relation to that particular Pope. So, to add to the universality conferred by canonisation, Malachy has an added universality of his own. So far as Ireland is concerned, he is eternally linked to the precious gift of independence which his sanctity ensured for the Church in his native land.

Perhaps the most significant comment in this context comes from the written work of St. Bernard of Clairvaux. Describing the impression given by Malachy as he carried out his reforms, St. Bernard says, ". . . one thought he was born only for his country; if you had seen him alone, living on his own, you would have thought he lived only in God and for Him."

St. Laurence O'Toole   1123–1180
14 November

When Henry II of England arrived in Ireland in 1171 to initiate the occupation of the country, he brought with him the most controversial authority in Irish history. This consisted of a Donation of Ireland to Henry II, allegedly signed by the English Pope Adrian IV in 1154. Adrian was dead by this time, but his successor, Alexander III, who was still alive at the time had signed a second Donation on the basis of Adrian's authority. These documents, regarded with great suspicion by many historians, seemed at the time sufficiently authentic to cause confusion since most of the Bishops, at least at first, accepted Henry however reluctantly. The first to entertain doubts and to question the motives and methods of Henry was the Archbishop of Dublin, Laurence O'Toole.

As time went on, Henry found this Bishop a constant thorn in his side. His attitude to him bore a striking similarity to his antipathy to Thomas à Becket, and led to a strangely similar result. In 1175, the Archbishop of Dublin came to England as an envoy to Henry. While he was saying Mass, he was felled with a club and barely survived. It has never been clarified who insti-

61

gated this incident, but the comparison with the assassination of Thomas à Becket, generally held to have been the work of the same monarch, has constantly been pointed out in historical accounts of Laurence O'Toole.

Laurence O'Toole was a prince of one of the oldest families in Ireland, with an ancestry dating back to a second century ancestor. His mother was an O'Byrne, the other of the two great families of Leinster. The King of Leinster at the time was Dermot MacMurrough, destined to pass into history as the "Judas" of Ireland, for it was he who obtained allies among the Norman Knights in his private quarrels and led to the invasion of Ireland. This monarch was married to a sister of Laurence O'Toole.

Laurence spent over twenty years at the famous Abbey of Glendalough, most of the time as Abbot. In 1161, by the consent of all, he was selected as Archbishop of Dublin. In that capacity, he was faced with major problems, the most pressing of which were the difficulties caused by the Ostmen, or descendants of the Vikings, who were hostile to the native Irish clergy, and the continuing criticism coming from the Norman hierarchy in Canterbury. In a few years, he had the added problems which came with the Norman invasion.

A superficial view of Irish history would be that the victory of the Irish king, Brian Boru, at the battle of Clontarf in 1014, had ended the Viking bid for empire, especially in Ireland. This was not totally correct, for the descendants of the Vikings held commanding positions in all the major cities of Ireland which, in fact, they had created. They were strongly represented in the Irish hierarchy, again in the cities. They were averse to accepting control by native Irish Bishops and had virtually turned to Canterbury as their legitimate superior See. They accepted its authority to consecrate their Bishops and in a variety of ways made it clear that they would prefer it if Canterbury took over control of the Irish Church.

Laurence O'Toole, a native Irish Bishop, had serious problems in Dublin, since this was by far the strongest centre of Viking influence. As it happened, the problem was solved in a way that neither he nor the Ostmen could foresee. The Norman invasion was so obviously an occupation that the Ostmen became rapidly disenchanted, especially when they saw that English policy included placing Normans in every important position in the Church. In this process, little or no distinction was made between Irish and Ostmen, in replacing candidates from Ireland. As a result, while Laurence O'Toole had immediate problems with Ostmen, his ultimate canonisation in 1225 was strongly supported by evidence from the Ostmen of Dublin.

His immediate policy to adjust relations with the Ostmen was completely in accordance with the sanctity which he displayed at all times, and which was to lead to his canonisation. He made of the Ostman foundation, Christ Church Cathedral, the central point of his Archdiocese. He spent hours there in devotion. He planned and carried out important extensions. He introduced the Augustinian Order and habit into the Cathedral, entered the community and adopted the habit of the Order. He persuaded Irish nobles, among them Dermot MacMurrough, to contribute to the great expansion of the Cathedral. Before long, the Ostmen were beginning to react favourably to the attitude of the Irish, led by Laurence O'Toole. The Norman invasion completed the process, and brought about the final rapprochement between the Irish and the descendants of the Vikings.

In 1166, Dermot MacMurrough, King of Leinster, brought on himself the wrath of several Irish princes, when he abducted Dervorgilla, wife of O'Rourke, Prince of Brefni. In a short time, they had totally defeated him and he took himself off to England to seek allies. He found them by offering his daughter, Eva, as bride to Richard de Clare, known as Strongbow, together with the succession to the Kingdom of Leinster. Strongbow arrived in Ireland in 1169 with the first group of Normans and set in train eight centuries of Irish history.

The hereditary Ard-Ri, High King of Ireland, was Roderick O'Connor, destined in fact to be the last of the long line of High Kings. He chose Laurence O'Toole as the most suitable man to act as mediator, especially in view of his relationship with Mac-Murrough who was the brother-in-law of the Archbishop. It so happened that a massacre of citizens by the Normans took place in the streets of Dublin, while the negotiations were going on. Laurence O'Toole was so horrified that he reported without delay to the High King that nothing short of a national campaign to evict the invaders would meet the case. In the event, the High King temporised and lost the initiative.

From this time on, the Archbishop had serious doubts about the whole Norman project. Even when Henry II arrived in July 1171, armed with the controversial papal authority, it never seemed to Laurence O'Toole that the Norman intentions were quite what the Popes wished, if indeed the documents were genuine. As time went on, he became more and more convinced that this was not a temporary measure to stabilise affairs in Ireland but a permanent military occupation. Considering that in 1179 Pope Alexander III, one of the Popes who allegedly endorsed the invasion, appointed Laurence O'Toole as his Papal Legate to Ireland, there are good grounds for believing that the Pope himself had realised that there was something suspicious about Norman intentions. For by the time the Pope appointed him, it was already widely known, and known to the Pope, that Laurence O'Toole was Henry II's greatest and most outspoken opponent in Ireland. His appointment, therefore, as Papal Legate could only mean that the Pope himself endorsed his opposition to Henry.

Laurence O'Toole acted with great courage on his return to Ireland. He used his authority as Papal Legate to carry out swift reforms in the Church. These reforms involved severe penalties against Norman nominees. In spite of the displeasure of Henry, he used his authority to report more than one hundred of them to Rome for judgement by an ecclesiastical court. It can well be imagined that he was no longer the ideal person to act as mediator between the King of England and the High King of Ireland. Inevitably, when the High King chose him again to intercede with the English King, Henry refused to see him and, in fact, went off to France. Three weeks later, Laurence O'Toole followed him. Before he could try again to see Henry, he died at the monastery of Eu, in Normandy. It is in tribute to him that the point at which he landed is now known as St. Laurent.

From the moment of his death, reports of miracles around his tomb were constantly circulating. The monks of Eu considered him a saint from that moment, and it was they who pressed for his canonisation. The support from Ireland was immediate and spontaneous. The impact of his sanctity on those who knew him can be measured by the fact that his canonisation was widely supported, both in Ireland and in England, and by Irish, Vikings and Normans. This volume of support from among the Normans seems surprising considering the attitude he adopted in dealing with his various problems.

The improvement he created in relations with the Vikings has been described above. His outspoken criticism of King Henry II and his invasion of Ireland, made it unlikely that Normans would be among those who shared the veneration he created. In fact, it must be borne in mind that Henry II did not enjoy the complete support of the entire Norman clergy. He could hardly be described as the ideal Christian King. He was widely held to have organised the assassination of Thomas à Becket. He consistently challenged the universal authority of Rome and in other ways interfered with the independence of the hierarchy of England. Silent disapproval of his behaviour was very clearly shown by the massive support for the canonisation of Thomas à Becket. Norman support for the canonisation of Laurence O'Toole reflected a similar attitude. It can reasonably be assumed that Henry II did not regard support for the canonisation of these two Archbishops as anything but a severe rebuke to which he could not respond.

The judgement of Laurence O'Toole by posterity must take into account the troubled period in Ireland during his life. He emerged as the only real leader at the time. The High King of Ireland was strangely ineffectual, in that he failed to bring about a national unity, even at the time when the problem was a minor one and could easily have been dealt with. It was left to the saintly Archbishop to protect the Irish Church from attack, and to strive at the same time to preserve the integrity of Ireland. He has earned an illustrious place in Irish history, as the first leader who saw the threat to both the Irish Church and to the nation. His canonisation in 1225, forty-five years after his death, was a clear judgement by the Universal Church that all he did was consistent with all the requirements of a true saint. His remains are enshrined in an honoured place above the High Altar in the Abbey of Eu, where he died, and where his veneration ultimately led him to the honours of the altar.

Fearghal (Virgilius) of Salzburg   784
27 November

Fearghal is widely venerated in Southern Germany, Austria, Yugoslavia and in Northern Italy. He is better known by his latinised name, Virgilius, and this name is commonly bestowed on boys in those areas, in his memory.

He first attracted attention when he arrived at the Court of Pepin, the father of Charlemagne, accompanied by two other Irish monks, Dobdagrec and Sidonius. Pepin was so attracted by their learning that he kept them at his Court for two years. He then decided to send them to Duke Otillo of Bavaria who received them willingly. Virgilius was placed in charge of the diocese of Salzburg. In fact, he became Abbot of St. Peter's Salzburg and appointed Dobdagrec to carry out the episcopal duties.

Historians have frequently referred to disputes which arose between Virgilius and Boniface, the Apostle of Germany. Since Boniface was an Anglo-Saxon, from Crediton in Devon, it is often stated that these differences were due to anti-Irish prejudice on the part of Boniface. This is most improbable, since Boniface had to deal with many Irish monks and placed many of them in important positions. In fact, when Boniface was martyred in Frisia in 754, two of his companions, also martyred at the same time, were Irish monks, Eoban and Adalar.

The real reason for constant disputes was probably the question of Celtic practices which were in conflict with the rules laid down by the Holy See. It seems that at times Virgilius may have interpreted the rules in an unorthodox manner, in the judgement of Boniface, who made a major issue of these incidents on at least two occasions. Both of them were reported to Pope Zachary and, the second time, Boniface pressed for the excommunication of Virgilius.

The first case concerned a baptism in which incorrect Latin wording was apparently used. Virgilius took the view that this did not affect the validity of the sacrament. The second case concerned the advanced views of Virgilius concerning the universe, Virgilius holding that the world was round and that people might well be living in what would now be called the Antipodes. To the orthodox mind of Boniface, this put Virgilius in contempt of Holy Scripture. In both cases, the Pope decided in favour of Virgilius and, in fact, the Holy See later consecrated him as Archbishop of Salzburg.

The references to these incidents have tended to lessen the importance of the missionary work he carried out. He is called the Apostle of Carinthia which is the wide area of Southern Austria, North-East Italy and Yugoslavia. The Dukes of Carinthia had, like Pepin, a high regard for him. One of them, Chetimar, issued a coin which is the basis of a legend of special Irish interest.

This coin bore on one side the likeness of Virgilius, and on the other, of Rupert, who had laboured in Salzburg some seventy years before Virgilius and founded St. Peter's. More than one historian, including Colgan, believe Rupert to have been Irish. According to this tradition, he brought from Ireland his sister or niece, Erintrude, whom he placed as Abbess over the convent of Nonnberg, near Salzburg. This is the convent which became so widely known in recent years as the setting for much of the famous film and play, *The Sound of Music*.

Virgilius was canonised by Pope Gregory IX in 1233. He has little or no cult in Ireland and indeed is little known there. This is somewhat surprising, not only because Ireland has only five canonised saints, but also because it is clear that he was well known as an Irish monk in his mission. This fact obviously played a considerable part in his dealings with Boniface. Moreover, it was Virgilius who brought to those territories the veneration of St. Brigid of Kildare and St. Samthan of Clonbroney. Indeed, it is quite likely that the latter saint, an early nun in Ireland, is better known in Austria than she is in Ireland. Virgilius, or Fearghal, was undoubtedly one of those "Exiles for Christ" who played a considerable part in establishing the Golden Age and in earning for his native land the title of Island of Saints and Scholars.

Oliver Plunkett   1625–1681
1 July

When Oliver Plunkett was sent from Rome to Ireland as Primate in 1669, the parting words to him of a Polish priest in Rome were, "My Lord, you are now going to shed your blood for the Catholic Faith". Twelve years later, he became the last of those executed at Tyburn. In those years of service in Ireland, he underwent a martyrdom, inflicted upon him not only by those who eventually put him to death, but from his own people, to whom he had come to minister.

The conditions of life in Ireland were more complex at the time of his arrival, than they have ever been. It was a society within which, as he found to his cost, there were at least four specific groups, all of whom required the attention of the Primate, the Archbishop of Armagh. The recent history of the holders of that office would have daunted any but a man filled with the Holy Spirit.

The fate of his immediate predecessors gave some indication of the perils in which he walked. In 1587, Richard Creagh died in the Tower of London after eighteen years of imprisonment. The next one, Edmund McGauran, was murdered in Tulsk, in exile, in 1593. The next five died in exile. Oliver Plunkett was the next.

The first of the groups referred to above was, of course, the Catholic people of Ireland. After five centuries of occupation and incessant pressure to destroy their culture, the native Irish were virtually identical with the Catholic population – to them an Irishman was a Catholic. What that meant was that both as Irishmen and Catholics they had developed a complete distrust of the English Crown and of all those who bore its image in Ireland. All landlords, even Catholic ones, fell into that class. The Gaelic language was the badge of Irish culture. To them, an Irishman had to be Gaelic, Catholic and opposed to English influence. Oliver Plunkett belonged to one of the most prominent Catholic landowning families loyal to the Crown. They were Anglo-Irish, not Gaelic.

The second group was the Irish clergy, recruited almost entirely from the native Irish, who surveyed the new Archbishop from the same standpoint. In their case, however, there was an added problem, a very old one in Ireland, dating back to the time of St. Patrick himself. This was the relationship between Bishops and the Orders in monasteries. Ireland had never fully accepted the over-riding authority of Bishops. It can easily be imagined that Oliver Plunkett had trouble from the beginning in exerting his authority under those conditions.

The third group has passed into history as the Rapparees, or Tories. These were the descendants of the Irish dispossessed landowners, who kept up a continuous guerilla war against the Crown and its representatives in Ireland. They were, of course, Catholic and as such were a responsibility of the new Primate in his overall policy.

The fourth, and last of these groups, was the Anglo-Irish landlords, mostly Protestant, and loyal to the Crown. Their attitude to the new Archbishop was dictated more by his family background than by his religion. Indeed, he obtained considerable help from them, even in his pastoral tasks. It is to the credit of these Irish Protestants to place on record that an all-Protestant Court refused to find him guilty in Ireland of the charges on which he was finally martyred. Indeed, they made very severe comments on the nature and validity of the evidence given by disreputable witnesses for the prosecution.

A brief look at the background of Oliver Plunkett will show how his image, as it appeared to those among whom he worked, created problems which might not have affected another kind of Irishmen in the same appointment. For, tragically for him, unlike his predecessors listed above, whose sole problem was English policy, it was from within the Irish people that the hostility came to make his martyrdom possible.

Oliver Plunkett was born at Loughcrew, Co. Meath, and was closely related to several titled members of the nobility. One of these was the Earl of Fingal, another the Earl of Roscommon, who had gone over to the Church of England. Another of his relatives was a Bishop of Dublin. This family had succeeded in retaining their estates and even holding high office and, indeed, they have always been prominent in Irish affairs. Within living memory, one of this family was the Protestant Archbishop of Dublin. In another area of activity during the same period, the poet Joseph Mary Plunkett was executed in 1916 for his part in the Easter Rising.

Oliver was in his early teens when the Pope's representative in Ireland, Father Peter Scarampi, returned to Rome bringing with him five boys, including Oliver Plunkett and John Brennan, later to be a bishop in Ireland, and one of those who launched the first moves for Oliver's canonisation. In Rome, Oliver settled down to a scholarly existence, with no apparent intention of returning to Ireland. In 1669, when Oliver was forty-four years of age, Edmund O'Reilly, Archbishop of Armagh, died in exile, and Pope Clement IX chose Oliver Plunkett to succeed him. He was secretly consecrated in Ghent, Belgium that year on his way to Ireland. which he entered disguised as an Army captain, and using the name Brown. His immediate arrest was only averted through the influence of his Protestant kinsman, the Earl of Roscommon.

From that time onwards, his varying prestige among the various groups with whom he had to deal, began to have the impact which led inexorably to his martyrdom. He got help where he could least expect it. He never gained the full confidence of those from whom he should have received it. Sad to relate, it was from resentful meembers of the Religious Orders that the vicious propaganda was to come which led to the final tragedy of Oliver Plunkett.

As Archbishop of Armagh, he saw it as his clear duty to urge essential reforms on the religious. Discipline had broken down to an alarming extent, both in the Orders and among the secular Clergy. Personal lives were frequently scandalous. The administering of the Sacraments was far below the needs of the people. The monastic rules of the monks, mainly Franciscans and, to a lesser extent, Dominicans, were widely neglected. Before long, the Archbishop's determined and courageous reforms produced a number of priests who were disciplined by him in one way or another. It also produced the nucleus of the group of enemies intent on destroying him.

From this source came the rumours which circulated to drive the wedge between Oliver and the faithful. So it became widely said that he was too friendly with the Anglo-Irish, that he was, essentially, one of them himself. They saw no merit in the fact that he had increased tolerance towards the Catholics and had even obtained land, buildings and funds from Protestants to help his activities for the Catholic people. Malice knows no limits and an attempt was actually made to denounce him to the Pope. The worst accusation, and potentially the most damaging was that he obtained agreement from leading Rapparees to cease their warfare in return for freedom to leave Ireland. Having done that, so rumour had it, he had one of their leaders, Patrick Fleming, ambushed and killed.

This story was particularly damaging because it was so persistent. The truth, which was available at the time to those prepared to examine the facts, was so different from the rumour, that it must be concluded that the attacks on the Archbishop were deliberately contrived to produce the maximum effect. So far from there being any hostility between Oliver and the Rapparees, it has always been well known that he was held in the highest respect by them, and earned their gratitude on more than one occasion. Instead of denouncing them, he persuaded them to desist from their guerilla warfare and he arranged for their emigration with immunity. It speaks volumes for the manner in which he conducted his relations with them, that the most famous of them, Redmond O'Hanlon, devoted himself to the Archbishop's protection. Time and again, agents of the Crown decided to arrest Oliver, and O'Hanlon and his men swooped down and rescued him. In fact, it has often been said that one of the reasons why Oliver was finally taken out of Ireland for trial was that O'Hanlon would never allow him to be executed in Ireland. It is hard to believe, since O'Hanlon was the great hero of the Irish people, a sort of Robin Hood, that his admiration for the Archbishop was not in itself enough to counter the vicious propaganda which marred the image of Oliver Plunkett.

The Popish plot of Titus Oates, while it lasted, was sufficient to arouse anti-Catholic and anti-Irish sentiment to such a pitch that no prominent Catholic was safe while the monstrous fabrication lasted. According to the story, a large French army had been got ready to invade and very quickly the suspicion arose that Oliver Plunkett was deeply involved. The order went out to arrest the Archbishop and try him without delay. As has been described above, the Protestant Court in Ireland refused to find him guilty. The quality of justice at that time can be measured by the fact that his transfer to England was ordered so that he could be tried again and, it must be assumed, found guilty.

The grim realities of the campaign against the character of Oliver Plunkett are to be seen in the kind of witnesses and evidence prepared for his prosecution. It is sufficient to describe briefly a main witness. This was Florence MacMoyre, the last of a great Irish family, which had the distinction of being the hereditary keepers of the Book of Armagh, an Irish cultural treasure. He gave his evidence in the hope of a reward, which he never received. He then pawned his great family treasure for five pounds, returned to Ireland and in due course ended his life in an Irish prison.

The execution of Oliver Plunkett did not meet with general approval among non-Catholics in England and most certainly not in Ireland. Even the ruling clique in London were somewhat uneasy and it may have been this which led to an unusual sequel. It is commonly believed that a Royal Pardon was dispatched by the Monarch, declaring the Archbishop innocent of the charges. One version has it that it arrived too late, after the execution. Another has it that it arrived before the execution and somehow was held up long enough to be too late. This may have had something to do with the fact that Oliver Plunkett was the last to be executed at Tyburn.

Posterity, with the advantage of three centuries of hindsight, is in a better position to assess the true place in Irish history of Oliver Plunkett. The fact that he was not of native Irish stock is no longer relevant, if it ever was, especially since a long succession of Anglo-Irish Protestants have become Irish heroes in political struggles. At this stage, all Irishmen should accept the fact that his canonisation, the culmination of the most searching research process anywhere in the world, is the complete vindication of all his actions. He rose above the attacks on his character and succeeded in doing what might have totally discouraged a lesser man. He personally confirmed more than 10,000 Catholics, he raised the standards of the Clergy, he set up the machinery to ensure their proper education and he courageously faced up to those whose conduct was a scandalous threat to those standards. The sad sequel was that, of the nine witnesses, all Irish, for the Crown, four were priests suspended by the Archbishop for unpriestly behaviour.

The body of Oliver Plunkett lies in the Benedictine Abbey, Downside, in England. His head is displayed in Drogheda, and is a well-known centre for pilgrims. It was in his honour that Pope John Paul II made Drogheda the scene of what many felt was the most significant of his pronouncements to the people of Ireland and to the world, during his visit to Ireland in 1979.

The following Saints were recognised by various Popes, but never received canonisation.

Sedulius (Siadal)   5th century
12 February
   The legendary scholarship of Siadal is a clear indication that

schools of learning existed in Ireland before Patrick began his Mission. He founded a school of poetry in Athens and in 430 wrote his famous Christian epic *Carmen Paschale*. On the strength of this, he is known as the Christian Virgil.

His Irish origins have been recorded many times, particularly by Dicuil, the eighth century Irish scholar who speaks of "our own Sedulius". Other experts claim that the metrical structure of his verses is clearly Irish. In 1922, George Sigerson published an English translation of the *Carmen Paschale* and described it as the work of "Sedulius, the first Scholar-Saint of Erinn". There is some evidence that he may have been a disciple in Ireland of Ailbhe, the pre-Patrician Bishop of Emly (see p. 16).

In 494, a decree of the First Roman Council of the Church contained a phrase "honouring by signal praise the Paschal Work of the Venerable man, Sedulius".

Attracta (Adhracht) of Achonry   5th century
11 August

It is possible that Attracta was working for Christianity in Connaught before Brigid appeared on the scene. She founded the convent of Killaraght in Sligo and another in Roscommon. She is Patroness of the Diocese of Achonry and her cult is very strong and durable, especially in the west of Ireland.

Her name is popular among Irish girls. She is credited with exceptional powers of curing the sick and her convents were famous for hospitality and charity for the poor. The strength of the veneration in which she has been held for fourteen centuries is dramatically illustrated by the act of Pope Pius IX in 1829 when he personally authorised the Mass of St. Attracta on her feast day in the Diocese of Achonry.

This was the year in which the Catholic Emancipation Act in the British Isles was signed. This event was of major importance throughout the Catholic Church. The fact that the Pope chose this moment to honour an Irish Saint must indicate the strength of the cult of St. Attracta who appears to have been the only Irish saint honoured at that very significant time.

Gobnait of Ballyvourney, Co. Cork   6th century
11 February

Tradition has it that Gobnait was told by angels that she would find the place of her resurrection where nine white deer grazed. She found this place at Ballyvourney where she set up an Abbey with the help of St. Abban of Kilabban, Co. Meath. Her Well is still there and is an attraction for pilgrims.

A favourite legend concerning her is how she used her bees to drive off unwelcome visitors. Her wooden image was for centuries an object of great devotion and the churchyard at Ballyvourney contains crutches and other evidence of cures obtained through her intercession. Her name, appropriately enough, means Honey Bee.

More than one of the leading families of Munster have a traditional devotion to Gobnait. The O'Herlihys originally granted the land for her Abbey, and her wooden statue was in their keeping until the nineteenth century.

The devotion of the O'Sullivan Beare family may have been the reason why Pope Clement III honoured Gobnait in 1602 by authorising the Mass on her feast day. It was about that time that the Chieftains of Ireland were making a final struggle for independence and the entire Clan of the O'Sullivan Beares migrated to the North having dedicated their fortunes to Gobnait of Ballyvourney in a mass pilgrimage.

Tressan of Avenay, France   6th century
7 February

Said to have been one of six brothers and three sisters, all of whom laboured in the Diocese of Rheims. The most famous of these was Gibrian (v. page 117) the titular saint of St. Gibrian.

The devotion to Tressan is very strong and continuous in the Rheims area. He is the Patron Saint of Avenay. More than one thousand years after his death, Pope Clement VIII, who had honoured Gobnait of Ballyvourney, authorised the printing of an Office for the Irish Saint Tressan of Avenay.

Wendel of Tholey, Germany   6th century
21 October

Wendel is an outstanding example of an Irish saint whose identity has almost been lost. Even his name, frequently quoted as Wendelin, is German. The Diocese of Trier, where he is recorded as Irish, state that there are in the USA alone seventeen towns or villages named after him. Yet few of his devotees there are aware of his Irish origins. Wendell incidentally is a common American christian name. Indeed, a presidential candidate in the USA in 1940, was Wendell Wilkie.

He chose to set up his hermitage at Tholey near Trier. Later this became the Benedictine Abbey of Tholey. Tradition has it that so many miracles occurred at his death that a church was built on the spot to inter his body, and later the town of St. Wendel was set up there by one of the Holy Roman Emperors in the fourteenth century.

A missionary society in his name is now active. It is called the Society of the Divine Word Mission House of St. Wendel. In this case, as in many others, it should be noted that official recognition of this organisation also involved acceptance of the title "Saint" in his name.

Berthold of Chaumont   6th century
16 June

Berthold's Abbey in the Diocese of Rheims became the modern town of Chaumont. Many miracles occurred at his death and four centuries later a new monastery and church were established in his honour. Several Popes have granted indulgences to pilgrims at the Shrine of Berthold. In particular, Pope Nicholas VI in 1451 and Pope Paul II in 1466 honoured his memory in this way.

Etto (Ze) of Dompierre, Belgium   c. 670
10 July

In 1920, Cardinal Mercier, writing to the Bishops of Ireland who had sought his intercession of behalf of Ireland during the troubles, mentioned Etto as one of the Irish missionaries to whom Belgium owed a special debt of gratitude. Etto had worked in East Anglia with Fursey (v. p. 37), and accompanied him on a pilgrimage to Rome where he was consecrated Bishop.

He set up the Abbey of Fescan, near Dompierre and laboured as an Abbot Bishop. His cult started immediately after his death, in the whole region, and he is one of those traditional saints whose relics were accompanied by a mounted escort in processions.

In two distinct places, confraternities in the name of St. Ze (Etto) have been set up. They are both authorised in that name at Dompierre and Buinvilliers. Etto is a typical example of an Irish saint with no cult in Ireland, who continues to be venerated over a wide area outside Ireland. It is also worth noting that his Irish identity is clearly written into the records of the Diocese, although his Irish name is unknown.

Erhart of Ratisbon, Germany   c. 686
8 January

An Irish missionary Bishop in Bavaria. Many miracles are attributed to him, the most notable being the restoration of sight to a child whom he baptised. The child was Odilia who, in due course, was honoured as a Saint.

The devotion to the memory of Erhart is very strong indeed. It was demonstrated in a most remarkable way. A religious body of women was formed after his death, called the Erardinonnen (the Nuns of Erhart), who maintained a perpetual round of prayer at his crypt in Ratisbon until the Reformation. This Order and the devotion for which they were founded was sanctioned by Pope Leo IX.

Fridian of Lucca, Italy   588
18 March

Fridian was the subject of a remarkable tribute from Pope Gregory the Great, who paid public homage to the exemplary character of his life. He also stated categorically that Fridian had miraculously diverted a river to prevent ruin to the crops and lives of the people on its banks.

The Irishness of Fridian, also called Frigidian, has been called into question. However, he is quoted in many lists as Irish, and indeed his name, Frigidian, could well be Irish. Moreover, the history of the Order which bears his name reflects Irish traditions, and so was presumably founded by him.

He was the titular Saint of the Canons Regular of St. Fridian based in Lucca. In 1105, Pope Paschal II invited the Order to re-form the Canons Regular of the Lateran, according to the Rule of the Order in Lucca. There are grounds for saying that the Canons of St. Fridian followed a Rule which was imparted to them by one trained in the monastic schools of Ireland.

Historical records show that Lucca was an important centre of Irish influence in the Middle Ages, a tradition which was normally initiated by a prominent Irish missionary. It is also a fact of importance, in estimating the Irish traditions of the Canons Regular of St. Fridian, that since their association with the Canons Regular of the Lateran, that Order now claims St. Patrick and St. Brigid among its members. Fra. Tommasini, the great authority on Irish saints in Italy, considers that this is due to the Irish traditions of the Order from Lucca, founded in the name of St. Fridian.

Adamnan of Coldingham, Scotland   680
31 January

This is not the Adamnan who is famous for his biography of St. Columba of Iona. This Adamnan has been venerated principally in the South East of Scotland near Berwick. He established a reputation for the extreme rigour of his Rule, strict even beyond the traditions of Irish monasticism.

The Abbey of Coldingham was composed of both monks and nuns, and the presence of Adamnan was more conspicuous for that reason. He was constantly critical of what he called frivolous behaviour in the community and predicted that, unless the discipline became more suitable to a religious community, it would be destroyed by fire.

The Abbess, Ebba, who was a royal princess, was greatly troubled. She was a saintly woman, and is listed among the traditional saints of Britain. Adamnan assured her that the Abbey would not be destroyed in her lifetime. In fact, it was destroyed by fire shortly after her death in 683. Pope Leo XIII confirmed the feast day of St. Adamnan in 1897.

Concord of Lemniec, France   1120–1176
4 June

The story of Concord is one of the most remarkable in the whole history of Irish saints. He became Archbishop of Armagh in 1174 at one of the most critical periods in the history of Ireland and of the Church in Ireland. The invasion of the Normans was already developing into an occupation. At the same time, the native Irish clergy were under severe pressure both from the Norman Bishops led from Canterbury, and from the Ostmen, descendants of the Vikings, who were very strongly represented among the hierarchy in Ireland, especially in the big cities. At that time, Laurence O'Toole (v. Ch. 4) who was later canonised, was conducting a vigorous defence of Irish interests as Archbishop of Dublin.

In that situation, Conchobar Mac Conaille, the real name of Concord, went to Rome to plead for support from the Pope for the Irish cause. On his way back, he fell ill and died at Lemniec in the Diocese of Chambéry, France. Miracles took place immediately and Concord, as the local people have always called him, became the Patron of the entire countryside.

A Confraternity of St. Concord flourished for five centuries until, in 1671, Pope Clement X had it investigated and sanctioned it, accepting the name of St. Concord in its title. He also authorised a formal habit for the members. Later, in 1854, the body of Concord was exhumed by a Vatican Commission which found his brain incorrupt.

It was at this point apparently that Archbishop Dixon of

Armagh saw the account of this investigation in a French news-paper and first learned of this Irish saint. It is a sad commentary on the confused history of Ireland that the fate of a Primate of All-Ireland, and the widespread veneration he inspired, continued in France for seven centuries before it became common knowledge in Ireland itself. This lack of information was shared even by one of his own successors in the See of Patrick.

Shrines containing his relics are now maintained in the Sacred Heart Convent in Armagh, and in the Presentation Convent in Drogheda.

CHAPTER V

The Irish Martyrs

In 1896, the list of Irish Martyrs, drawn up by Father Denis Murphy, was published. On the 16th March 1915, Pope Benedict XV ratified the Decree for the Introduction of the Cause of these 259 Irish martyrs. The list has been reduced to 258 by the canonisation of Oliver Plunkett. Further information since 1896 has led to a new examination by priest-historians in Dublin. The revised list which is likely to result from their expert scrutiny will then be ready for the renewed progress of the Cause.

It should be pointed out that several names of Irishmen were included in the list of English Martyrs already examined by the Holy See. The following are definitely identified as Irish, and were accorded titles of sanctity by Pope Pius XI on 15 December 1929. A brief account of each of them is included in Chapter VI "Irish Causes".

1537	Venerable John Travers
1588	Blessed John Roche
1594	Blessed John Cornelius (O'Mahony)
	Blessed John Carey
	Blessed Patrick Salmon
1598	Venerable James Dowdall
1644	Blessed Ralph Corby
1679	Venerable Charles Mihan (Meehan or O'Mahony)

Here follows the complete list of Irish Martyrs as published in 1896.

Irish Confessors and Martyrs

1572

Edmund O'Donnell, Jesuit, first definitely recorded martyr for the faith in Ireland under Elizabeth; hanged, drawn and quartered, Cork, October 25.

1575
Conor Macuarta and Roger MacConnell, Franciscans at Armagh; flogged to death. Franciscan guardian, Fergal Ward, Armagh; hanged with his own girdle.

1576
Franciscans John Lochan, Donagh O'Rorke, Edmund Fitzsimon; hanged, Downpatrick.

1577
William Walsh, Cistercian Bishop of Meath; after imprisonment, died in exile at Alcala. Thaddeus O'Daly, Franciscan; hanged, drawn and quartered at Limerick. Bystanders reported that his head when severed from his body distinctly spoke the words: "Lord show me Thy ways". John O'Dowd; for refusing to reveal a confession, put to death, his skull compressed with a twisted cord.

1579
Patrick O'Healy, Franciscan Bishop of Mayo who said he could not barter his faith for life or honours; his brother Franciscan Cornelius O'Rorke; tortured and hanged, Killmallock. Cistercian abbot and brethren, Mainsternenay, County Limerick; slain.

1580
Lawrence O'Moore, secular priest; tortured and hanged, Smerwick. William Walsh and Oliver Plunkett, laymen; executed with O'Moore. Eugene Cronin, secular priest; executed, Dublin. John Kieran of Tuam, Premonstratensian; hanged. Galasius O'Cullenan, Cistern abbot of Boyle; hanged, Dublin. Daniel O'Neilan, Franciscan; fastened around the waist with a rope and with weights tied to his feet was first thrown from one of the town gates at Youghal and then, fastened to a mill wheel was torn to pieces.

1581
Richard French, secular priest, died in prison, Wexford. Nicholas Fitzgerald, Cistercian; hanged, drawn and quartered in Dublin. Matthew Lamport, Wexford layman; hanged for harbouring a Jesuit. Robert Meyler, Edward Cheevers, John O'Lahy, Patrick Canavan, all Wexford laymen; hanged for conveying priests to France. Patrick Hayes, ship owner of Wexford; charged with aiding bishops, priests and others, died on release from prison.

Maurice Eustace, nobleman and Jesuit novice in Flanders against his father's bitter opposition, returned as a lay apostle in Ireland. Informed on by his servant, he was arrested for "high treason". If he would but accept the reformed religion, the Protestant archbishop of Dublin offered him his daughter in marriage and a large dowry. Unshaken by bribery or persecution he was hanged, drawn and quartered. Daniel Sutton, John Sutton, Robert Sherlock, Robert Fitzgerald, William Wogan, laymen; executed, Dublin, May 26. Walter Aylmer, Thomas Eustace, son Christopher, and brother Walter, laymen; hanged, Dublin.

1582
Aneas Penny, parish priest, Killagh; slain by soldiers while saying Mass. Philip O'Shea, Maurice O'Scanlon and Daniel Hanrahan, Franciscans; slain at Lislactin. Charles MacGoran, Roger O'Donnellan, Peter O'Quillan, Patrick McKenna, James Pillan and Roger O'Hanlon, Franciscans; died in prison, Dublin Castle. Phelim O'Hara, Franciscan lay brother; strangled before the altar. Henry Delahyde, Franciscan lay brother; suffered with O'Hara. Thaddeus O'Meran, Franciscan guardian of Emiscorthy; tortured to death.

1584
Dermot O'Hurly, bishop, tortured and hanged, Dublin. He had studied at Rheims, Louvain and Rome where he was consecrated bishop of Cashel. Intercepted on the way and committed to Dublin Castle, he was tied to a tree in Stephens Green where his clothing, even his body was saturated with oil and alcohol, his legs encased in boots filled with oil and salt. Lighting a fire beneath him, alternately they quenched and lighted the flames, prolonging his torture for four days. All this time he prayed "Jesus, have mercy on me" and steadfastly refused to deny his faith. He was finally removed by his torturers who pulled off his boots, stripping the flesh from his bones and so returned him to prison. He was hanged near Stephen's Green, Dublin. Prior and brethren, Graiguenamanagh, Cistercians; slain. Franciscan John O'Daly; trampled to death by cavalry. John O'Grady, secular priest, executed. Thaddeus Clancey, Ballyrobert, layman; beheaded. Eleanor Birmingham, laywoman, the only recorded woman sufferer for the faith during the times of Henry and Elizabeth; died in Dublin prison.

1585
Maurice Kenraghty, secular priest, taken by Ormond, was

chained to one Patrick Grant and imprisoned at Clonnel. A local Catholic, Victor White, bribed the jailor to release him overnight to say Mass and give Communion on Passion Sunday, which the jailor did and informed the authorities who arrested all at Mass. Father Kenraghty escaped but later gave himself up to save White's life. He was hanged as a traitor and his head was impaled in the Clonnel market place. Patrick O'Connor and Malachy O'Kelly, Cistercians; hanged, drawn and quartered at Boyle.

1586
Richard Creagh, bishop of Armagh; died, after eighteen years imprisonment, Tower of London. Donagh O'Hurley, Franciscan sacristan, Muckross Convent; tortured to death.

1587
Murtagh O'Brien, bishop of Emly; died in Dublin prison. John Cornelius, Franciscan of Askeaton; died under torture.

1588
Dermot O'Mulrony, guardian, and two brother Franciscans; beheaded at Galbally, County Limerick. John O'Molloy, Cornelius O'Doherty, Geoffrey O'Farrel, Franciscans, hanged, drawn and quartered at Abbeyleix. Thaddeus O'Boyle, guardian, Franciscan Convent, Donegal; killed by English soldiers. Peter Meyler, layman; executed at Galway or Wexford on his way from Spain.

1589
Patrick O'Brady (or Ward), Franciscan prior and six friars; slain in Monastery of Monaghan. Uncertainty of date.

1590
Matthew O'Leyn, Franciscan of Kilcrea Convent, Muskerry; killed by English soldiers. Christopher Roche, Wexford layman; killed by torture, London.

1591
Franciscans Terence Magennis, Manus O'Fury, Loughlan Mac-Keagh; died in prison. Michael Fitzsimmon, layman of Fingall; put to death.

1593
Edmund MacGauran, bishop of Armagh; slain at Tulsk.

1594

Andrew Stritch, secular priest; died in prison, Dublin.

1596

Bernard Moriarty, secular priest, vicar-general; his thighs broken by soldiers, died in prison, Dublin.

1597

John Stephens, secular priest, County Wicklow; convicted of saying Mass, hanged and quartered. Walter Fernan, priest; torn on rack, Dublin.

1599

George Power, secular-priest, vicar-general of Ossory; died in prison, Dublin.

1600

John Walsh, vicar-general, Dublin; died in prison at Chester. Nicholas Young, secular priest of Trim; died in Dublin Castle. Thomas MacGrath, layman; beheaded.

1601

Raymond O'Gallagher, bishop of Derry; slain. Daniel Molony, secular priest, vicar-general of Killaloe; died under torture, Dublin Castle. John O'Kelly, Connacht priest; died in prison. Donagh O'Cronin, secular priest, cleric; hanged, drawn and quartered, Cork. Brian Murchertagh, secular priest, archdeacon of Clonfert; died in prison, Dublin. Donagh O'Falvey, secular priest; hanged, Cork.

1602

Dominic Collins, Jesuit lay brother; hanged, Cork. As he was led out to execution, his hands tied behind his back, a halter about his neck, he exhorted the faithful, "Look up to heaven and, worthy descendants of your ancestors who ever constantly professed it, hold fast to that faith for which I am this day to die." He was not allowed to hang long on the gallows by his executioners who cut open his breast and, taking out his heart, held it up to the view of the people, uttering the usual "God save the Queen".

1603

Eugene MacEgan, bishop of Ross; slain. Patrick Brown, convert, alderman of Dublin; died in prison. Dominican communities, 21 members at Coleraine, 32 members at Derry; put to death at unknown date in reign of Elizabeth.

1606

Bernard O'Carolan, secular priest; hanged in Dublin. Cistercians of Assaroe, Donegal, Eugene O'Gallagher, abbot, and Bernard O'Trever, prior; slain by soldiers. John Burke, lord of Brittas, layman; hanged.

1607

John O'Luin (O'Lynn), Dominican; hanged at Derry.

1608

Donagh O'Luin, brother of John O'Luin (1607), Dominican prior at Derry; hanged and quartered there.

1609

Donagh MacCreid, secular priest; hanged, Coleraine.

1610

John Lune (Lyng) of Wexford, secular priest; hanged and quartered, Dublin.

1612

Franciscan Cornelius O'Devany, bishop of Down and Connor and one of those who gathered information on Ireland's martyrs up until his own time; hanged, Dublin. Catholics lined his route to the gallows to beg his blessing even as Protestant clergymen made last efforts to turn him from the faith. He kissed the gallows and turned to exhort the Catholics to constancy whereupon he was thrown off, cut down alive and quartered. Patrick O'Loughran, secular priest, hanged with Bishop O'Devany.

1614

William MacGallen, Dominican; executed at Coleraine.

1615

Loughlin O'Laverty, secular priest; hanged, Derry. Brian O'Neil, Art O'Neil, Rory O'Cane, Godfrey O'Kane and Alexander Mac-Sorley, laymen; hanged with O'Laverty at Derry.

1617

Thomas Fitzgerald, Franciscan commisary and visitator of the Irish province, died in Dublin prison. Franciscan John Honan (MacConnan), Connacht; tortured, hanged, drawn and quartered, Dublin.

1618

Patrick O'Deery, secular priest; hanged, Derry.

1620

James Eustace, Cistercian; hanged and quartered.

1622

John O'Cahan, Franciscan, Buttevant convent; died in prison, Limerick.

1628

Edmund Dungan, bishop of Down and Connor; died in Dublin Castle.

1642

Philip Clearay of Raphoe (?) secular priest; slain. Cistercian Malachy Sheil; hanged Newry. Peter O'Higgin, Dominican prior of Naas; hanged Dublin, March 24. Cormac MacEgan, Dominican lay brother; hanged. Raymond Keogh, Dominican of Roscommon priory; hanged (1643?). Stephen Petit, Dominican subprior, Mullingar; shot while hearing confessions on the battlefield. Hilary Conroy, Franciscan of Elphin; hanged Castlecoote. Fulgentius Jordan Augustinian; hanged. Friar Thomas, Carmelite; hanged July 6, Drogheda. Friar Angelus, Carmelite; killed Drogheda.

1643

Edmund Mulligan, Cistercian; slain near Clones by soldiers. Francis O'Mahony, Franciscan guardian at Cork; tortured and hanged, regained consciousness, was again hanged by his girdle. Peter, Carmelite lay brother; hanged Dublin.

1644

Cornelius O'Connor and Eugene O'Daly, Trinitarians returning from France; drowned at sea by Puritans. Hugh McMahon, Ulster noble, layman; executed, Tyburn, November 22.

1645

Patriot archbishop of Tuam, Malachy O'Queely, his priest secretary Tadgh O'Connell, and Augustine O'Higgin, both Augustinians; executed after the battle of Sligo, October 26. Henry White, secular priest, aged 80; hanged, Racconnell, Westmeath. Christopher Dunlevy, Franciscan; died at Newgate, London. Conor McGuire, Baron of Inniskillen, layman; hanged, drawn and quartered, Tyburn, February 20.

1647

Theobald Stapleton, founder of the college for the Irish at Madrid and former rector of the Irish college at Seville, secular priest, chancellor of the church of Cashel; stabbed while giving Communion. Theobald Stapleton (misnamed Edward) and Thomas Morrissey, secular priests, vicars choral; killed in Cashel massacre of 2,000 Irish. Richard Barry, Dominican prior; killed in Cashel massacre. John O'Flaverty, Dominican; killed, Coleraine. Nicholas Wogan, Franciscan; hanged Dublin. Richard Butler, Franciscan, and James Saul, lay brother; killed in Cashel massacre. William Hickey, Franciscan of Adair convent; slain. William Boynton, Jesuit; killed in Cashel massacre. Elizabeth Carney and Margaret of Cashel, laywomen; killed in Cashel massacre.

1648

Gerald Fitzgibben, Dominican cleric and David Fox, Dominican lay brother; killed at Killmallock. Donal O'Neaghton, Dominican lay brother, Roscommon priory; killed. James Reilly, Dominican priest and poet; killed near Clonmel.

1649

Thomas Bath, secular priest, Dominic Dillon and Richard Overton, Dominicans, Peter Taafe, Augustinian, John Bath, Jesuit, and brother Thomas; all killed in Drogheda massacre of 3,000 men, women and children. Brian Gormley, Franciscan; hanged, Drogheda. Richard Synnot, John Esmond, Paul Synnot, Raymond Stafford and Peter Stafford, Franciscans, and James Cheevers and Joseph Rochford, lay brothers; killed in Wexford massacre in which 2,000 Irish perished. Eugene O'Teevan (O'Lemon?), Franciscan; killed in Donegal convent (1650?). Robert Netterville, Jesuit; beaten to death with sticks, Drogheda. Peter Costelloe, Dominican of Staid; killed.

1650

Boetius Egan, Franciscan bishop of Ross; taken by Broghill, his hands and feet cut off; hanged at Carrigadrohid. Herber Mc-Mahon, bishop of Clogher; hanged, Inniskillen, September 17. Francis Fitzgerald, Franciscan; died in prison, Cork. Anthony Hussey, Franciscan; hanged Mullingar. Neilan Loughran, Franciscan; killed, Ulster.

1651

Terence Albert O'Brien, Dominican bishop of Emly; hanged, and head hacked off and impaled on St. John's Gate at Limerick. The pectoral cross which he took off and handed to his mother at the gallows is still preserved in the Dominican priory in Limerick. Roger Normoyle, secular priest, County Claire; hanged. Hugh Carrighy, secular priest; hanged with Normoyle, October 12. Myler McGrath, Father Michael of the Rosary, Dominican; hanged at Clonmel. Laurance and Bernard O'Farrell, Dominicans; killed, Longford. Ambrose O'Cahill, Dominican; killed, Cork. Edmund O'Beirne, Dominican; hanged, Jamestown. James Woulfe, Dominican; hanged after siege of Limerick. Gerard Dillon, Dominican; died in prison, York. James Moran and Donough Niger, Dominican lay brothers; killed. William O'Connor, Dominican; killed, Clonmel. John O'Cullen, Dominican of Athenry convent; hanged, Limerick. Thomas O'Higgin, Dominican; hanged, Clonmel. Denis O'Neilan, Franciscan; hanged, Inchicronin. Tadgh O'Caraghy, Franciscan; hanged, Ennis. Jeremiah MacInerny and Daniel MacClanchy, Franciscan; lay brothers; hanged, Quin. Roger MacNamara, Franciscan; killed near Quin. Anthony O'Bruadair, Franciscan cleric; hanged, Turlevachan, County Galway. Donough Serenen, Augustinian; hanged. Raymond O'Malley and Thomas Tully, Augustinians, and Thomas Deir, lay brother; hanged (or 1652). Dominic Fanning, alderman and mayor of Limerick; Daniel O'Higgin, physician; Thomas Stritch, former mayor; Major General Patrick Purcell; Geoffrey Galway, member of Parliament for Limerick in 1634; Geoffrey Baron, nephew of Franciscan Luke Wadding, member of the Supreme Council and agent of the Irish Confederation to France, who, having obtained permission to dress for his execution, triumphantly climbed the steps of the gallows in white taffetie; all laymen; hanged after the siege of Limerick, October 29–30. Donough O'Brien, nobleman, layman; burned alive by Parliamentarians, County Clare. James, Bernard and Daniel O'Brien, brothers, laymen; hanged Nenagh. Louis O'Farral, layman; died in prison, Athlone.

1652

Eugene O'Cahan, high born youth of Thomond, Franciscan guardian of Askeaton, studied in Rome, taught philosophy in Naples, returned to Ireland in 1641; taken prisoner and beaten, hanged in County Cork. Brian Fitzpatrick, secular priest of Ossory; suffered for the faith. Philip Flatisbury, Franciscan; hanged, New Ross. Francis O'Sullivan, Franciscan provincial; shot near Derrynane. Anthony O'Feral, Franciscan; killed, County Roscommon. John Ferall, Franciscan; killed, County Roscommon. Walter Walsh, Franciscan; died in prison, Dublin. Donough O'Kennedy, Augustian, hanged. Tadhg O'Connor, Sligo layman; hanged, Boyle. John O'Connor, Kerry layman; hanged, Tralee. Bernard MacBriody, layman, hanged. Edmund Butler, layman, son of Lord Mount-Garret; hanged, Dublin. Brigid D'Arcy, wife of Florence Fitzpatrick, laywoman; burned at the stake.

1653

Daniel Delaney, secular priest, Arklow; tied to a horse's tail, dragged to Gorey, hanged. Daniel O'Brien, secular priest, dean of Ferns; suffered with Delaney. Luke Bergin, Cistercian of Baltinglass; hanged with O'Brien and Delaney. David Roche, Dominican of Glenworth; sold as a slave to West Indies plantations in St. Kitts, died in captivity. Brian O'Kelly, Dominican lay brother; hanged Galway. Tadhg Moriarty, Dominican prior of Tralee; hanged, Killarney. Hugh MacGoill, Dominican, executed, Waterford. John Kearney, Franciscan; hanged, Clonmel. Theobald de Burgo, third viscount Mayo, layman; shot, Galway. Sir Phemil O'Neill, layman; hanged, drawn and quartered, Dublin. Honoria Magan and Honoria de Burgo, Dominican tertiaries; died of hardships while in flight from Puritan soldiers.

1654

William Tirry, Augustinian; hanged, Clonmel, May 12.

1655

William Lynch, Dominican of Straid; hanged (before 1655).

1656

Fiacre Tobin, Capuchin; died in captivity, Kinsale.

1659
Hugh MacKeon, Franciscan; died on release from jail (after 1659).

1661
Brian MacGiolla Choinne, Franciscan; died in captivity, Galway.

1669
Raymond O'Moore, Dominican; died in prison, Dublin.

1680
Peter Talbot, archbishop of Dublin; died in prison.

1681
(Blessed Oliver Plunkett, in separate listing.)

1686
Felix O'Connor, Dominican; died in jail, Sligo, about 1686.

1703
John Keating, Dominican; died in prison, Dublin.

1704
Clement MacColgan, Dominican; died in Derry jail.

1707
Daniel MacDonnell, Dominican; died in Galway jail.

1708
Felix MacDonnell, Dominican; died in prison, Dublin.

1710
John Baptist Dowdall, Capuchin; died in prison, London.

1711
Father O'Hegarty (baptismal name unknown) secular priest; killed according to tradition by heretics near Buncrana.

1713
Dominic Egan, Dominican; died in prison.

Denis Murphy; *Catholic Encyclopedia*; *New Catholic Encyclopedia*; McManus; Brennen, p. 16.

CHAPTER VI

Irish Causes

It has often been remarked that the Irish people are less impressed than they might be by the process of canonisation as it affects their own saints. There are many indications that the long history of veneration of their traditional saints is something with which those who were canonised cannot compete in the public estimation of departed Servants of God.

There are only five canonised Irish saints, Sillao, Malachy, Laurence O'Toole, Virgilius, Oliver Plunkett. It is doubtful if a majority of the Irish people could with any certainty say who they are. It is still more doubtful if a quarter of the people could quote them in the correct order of canonisation. It is almost certain that very few indeed could name two of them in particular. These are Sillao of Lucca, canonised by Pope Lucius III in 1183, and Virgilius of Salzburg (Fearghal) canonised by Pope Gregory IX in 1233.

The indifference to canonised saints cannot be dismissed as a phenomenon among the mass of the faithful. It is nationwide and exists at all levels. The ignorance about Virgilius is reflected even in announcements in the National Press of Ireland which more often than not state that Oliver Plunkett was the first canonised Irish saint since Laurence O'Toole. At the time of the Pope's visit to Ireland, an Irish writer in a leading English Catholic weekly informed readers that there are only two canonised Irish saints, Laurence O'Toole and Oliver Plunkett.

On the face of it, the indications are that Irish people are not interested in saints. This is not correct. Still less is it correct to say that they are not interested in Irish saints. The truth is that they are primarily interested in saints who are the object of the veneration, within Ireland, of Irish people. In the Irish tradition, the validity of sanctity in Ireland, is imparted almost entirely by the strength and durability of a cult within Ireland, and sustained by Irish people.

This explains why outstanding Irish people who are venerated outside Ireland are devoid of any real cult in Ireland itself. Virgilius of Salzburg was a distinguished Irishman. His cult and his canonisation are the concern of the faithful in Austria. He is not an Irish saint in the tradition of those venerated in Ireland. Veneration, at least in Ireland, is a very local matter and is confined to Ireland itself.

Something of the same feeling has to a greater or less extent affected total acceptance of all of the Irishmen so far canonised. The first of these was Sillao of Lucca, canonised in 1183 followed by Malachy, in 1190. Their sanctity and services to the Church in Ireland are acknowledged. However, their cause was pursued outside Ireland by those among whom they died. By chance, the next of the group, Laurence O'Toole, also died abroad and his cause was promoted by the monks of Eu in Normandy where he died. The next was of course Virgilius of Salzburg.

Of the five, the last, Oliver Plunkett, canonised by Pope Paul VI in 1975, is the only one whose cause could be said to have been promoted from within Ireland. In his case, however, there were serious limitations to the strength of the veneration which is so evident in the case of many of the traditional saints. Oliver Plunkett was never fully accepted as one of the native Irish, a fact of supreme importance in his time. It took 300 years before a miracle, not in Ireland but in an Italian hospital, finally decided the issue of his canonisation.

The attitude of the Irish people to their great saints can only be understood against the background of Irish history. It is sufficient to say that even St. Patrick was clearly not accepted for many centuries to the same extent as his successors, and partly at least because he was not Irish. Of the countless names in various lists of saints following his Mission, not one bore the name of Patrick. Nor was Patrick a common Christian name for boys, and the first prominent Irishman to bear the name for twelve centuries after Patrick's death, was Patrick Sarsfield. It was the Reformation which restored Patrick to his rightful place as the Apostle of Ireland.

Clearly the spontaneity which the Irish people are likely to display in pressing the cause of an Irish Servant of God will depend on the extent to which it is an issue of purely Irish Faith. Nowhere is this more evident than in the list of Irish Causes with which this chapter is concerned. Tadhg MacCarthy has been dead for 500 years. His cause is moving very slowly. Matt Talbot died in 1925. His cause is a living issue among Irish people. The difference is that Tadhg MacCarthy died in Italy and so his cult is principally there. Matt Talbot lived and died in Dublin. His cult belongs in Ireland.

Obviously there are issues important to Irish people in the selection of the objects of their veneration. To say that they are indifferent to canonisation is not really the story. To them, an Irish saint is one who is not only one of them, but is essentially supported by an Irish cult. His saintly life belongs to the Irish people. If not, he may still be a saint, but in the fullest sense he is not an Irish saint. He may be an Irishman venerated as a saint. It is important to know exactly where he is venerated and where the process began.

There are eighteen causes which concern Irish people. Of these, one began in France, two in Czecho-Slovakia, eight in England, one in Africa and another belongs primarily to Belgium. There are, therefore, five causes which are totally promoted from within Ireland. In that curious system of selection which is part of popular tradition, it is from within that group of five that the Irish people would most hope to see the next canonised Irish saint.

Tadhg MacCarthy   1455–1492
24 October

The cause of Tadhg MacCarthy is the oldest of existing Irish causes. From the time of his death in 1492, he has been venerated in Ivrea, in Savoy, and was beatified in 1895 by Pope Leo XIII. The promotion of his cause comes from the diocese of Cork and the Italian diocese of Ivrea where, incidentally, his remains lie in the cathedral under the high altar and are the object of continued veneration.

The lineage of the MacCarthys goes back to a King of Munster in the third century. This family was the most prominent of all Southern Irish families and inevitably they were immediately involved in resistance to the seizure of lands by the barons of Henry II of England. In their case, this led to centuries of warfare with the Norman Fitzgeralds.

Some idea of the situation created as time went on can be gauged from the fact that the leading figure perhaps in all Ireland was the Fitzgerald, Earl of Kildare. This was the noble who burned down the cathedral of Cashel. His apology for this was that he thought the archbishop, David Creagh, was inside it. It is not hard to imagine that such a man would react immediately when he heard that Pope Sixtus IV had consecrated Tadhg MacCarthy as bishop of Ross.

Fitzgerald contrived to place a rival claimant in the post with the result that Tadhg found it occupied on his return from Rome. The death of Sixtus IV at the same time gave Tadhg's enemies the opportunity to denounce him to the new Pope Innocent VIII who, completely deceived and disturbed by what he read, promptly excommunicated Tadhg who requested that a full enquiry should be held. On the basis of this, the same Pope issued three Bulls which totally exonerated Tadhg and appointed him to the bishopric of Cork and Cloyne.

The Fitzgeralds still opposed him and refused to surrender the property of the See, or to allow him to occupy it. This time, the same Pope who, four years earlier, had excommunicated Tadhg on the evidence of the Fitzgeralds, issued a fourth and final document, so strongly worded that the Fitzgeralds ceased all harassment of Tadhg, who set out from Rome to assume his appointment.

He travelled as a humble pilgrim and stayed overnight in the hospice at Ivrea, maintained for pilgrims by the Canons of St. Ursus of Ivrea, who, incidentally, is the Irish patron of this part of Italy.

At dawn, Tadhg was found dead. Tradition has it that the bishop of Ivrea had been disturbed all the night by a vivid dream of a bishop, unknown to him, being taken into heaven. The discovery, therefore, in Tadhg's possession, of a bishop's ring and other evidence of his station, made this dream the first of a long series of miracles connected with him. Numerous cures were reported at his tomb and his cult has been continuous ever since.

John Travers   1539
13 July

John Travers was the first Irishman to be tried in England and martyred at the very beginning of the Reformation. Details of the date and place of his birth are lacking and, indeed, it was only the fact of his being tried that brought him into prominence, during the same period as the trial and execution of Thomas More and John Fisher.

He was Chancellor of St. Patrick's Cathedral in Dublin, and enjoyed the reputation of being a considerable scholar. He produced what must have been one of the earliest works on the question of the Supremacy, the issue on which Henry VIII effectively launched the Reformation. John Travers made the case entirely in favour of papal supremacy and was immediately arrested, tried and executed. He seems to have been the only one listed among the English martyrs who was executed in Dublin.

An alleged miracle associated with him is worth recording since it has been several times recounted. According to these accounts, in answer to the Judge's question as to whether he wrote the book on which he was tried, he held up three fingers which, he said, had written it, and which should not be condemned. It is a persistent part of his story that all efforts to burn or otherwise destroy these fingers failed. It should, however, be admitted that details of his life are scanty, and the evidence for this miracle is equally so.

His cause is still proceeding. He was declared Venerable by Pope Pius XI on 15 December 1929.

John Cornelius of Bodmin, Cornwall   1594
Patrick Salmon
John Carey
4 July

All three of these were beatified by Pope Pius XI in 1929, along with the English martyrs. Patrick Salmon and John Carey were born in Dublin. John Cornelius, whose real name seems to have been O'Mahony, was born in Bodmin of Irish parents. He is not the only one who is listed under an assumed name among the English martyrs. The reason for this is that Irish names were so often an indication of Catholic affiliations.

He went overseas to study at Rheims and was ordained in Rome. He returned to England and for ten years he conducted his priestly mission and was finally arrested at Chideock Castle, the home of the Arundells. It is said that one of the family, Thomas Bosgrave, gave him his hat out of respect for his position as he expressed it. This was interpreted as collusion and he was also arrested and martyred on the same day. He is now also beatified.

The two Irish servants, Salmon and Carey, were taken off at the same time. They were tried and condemned at Dorchester and, along with Bosgrave, they were hanged. John Cornelius, considered more guilty since he was a priest, and what was worse, a Jesuit on his own admission, was hanged, drawn and quartered. All four were offered a reprieve if they would recant. On their refusal, the sentences were duly carried out.

James Dowdall   1598
13 August

Like so many others martyred in England, there are very few biographical details of James Dowdall. It is not known when he was born, nor precisely where, although it was clear that he was Irish, either from Drogheda or Wexford. He was a merchant trading between Ireland and the continent and, on his way back from France to Ireland, was driven on to the Devonshire coast. He was detained and questioned. He refused to accept the Queen's Supremacy. He went through the usual testing on the rack, but maintained his refusal and was executed on 13 August 1598.

He was declared Venerable by Pope Pius XI on 15 December 1929, and his cause continues.

John Roche   1588
28 August
John Roche was the servant of an English gentlewoman, Margaret Ward of Congleton, Cheshire. While living as a companion in a London home, Margaret Ward smuggled a rope into the Bridewell prison to assist a priest, Richard Watson, to escape. In trying to do so, he broke an arm and a leg. It seems that John Roche, by exchanging clothes with him, got him away but was himself arrested. Both he and Margaret Ward were promised immunity if they would say where the priest was and if they would accept the Protestant Faith. They steadfastly refused both conditions and were executed on 28 August 1588. They were both beatified with the English martyrs by Pope Pius XI in 1929.

Patrick Fleming, OSF   1599–1631
7 November
This Irish Franciscan would certainly have passed into Irish history for the monumental service he gave to the preservation of Irish culture. As it happens, he is also entitled to such a place as a martyr to the faith and as one whose cause for sanctification is now in progress. His cause was opened in 1903.

In the tragic times in which he lived, an Irish candidate for the priesthood had to undergo many hazards to enter training and still more to administer to the faithful. In the case of Patrick Fleming, he was only fourteen when he joined his uncle, Father Christopher Cusack, rector of St. Patrick's College, Douai. Five years later, he became a Franciscan at the Irish College of St. Anthony in Louvain. He was finally ordained at the Irish Franciscan College in Rome, at that time under the rule of Father Luke Wadding.

Father Wadding was one of the most powerful Irishmen of his time. Living in Rome, he was in an important position, for he was able to organise all kinds of services to Ireland, and especially to the Church, which were quite impossible for any Irishman at home. It was largely due to Father Wadding, for example, that much of the information regarding the old Irish missionaries in Europe was brought to light. It was he also who principally arranged facilities for Irishmen to study abroad for the priesthood. It was he again who was able very often to keep the Holy See accurately informed of what was currently happening to the Faith in Ireland.

It happened at that time that Michael O'Clery, a Franciscan laybrother and three collaborators were quietly gathering material for a massive history of Ireland and its culture, to be published as the Annals of the Four Masters. Quite naturally, Father Wadding was interested and active in finding suitable candidates to help in gathering material in various parts of Europe. Patrick Fleming was chosen to carry out this research task, in the course of which he visited the great Irish monasteries, Bobbio, St. Gall, the famous chain of Irish Abbeys centred at Ratisbon and many others. In fact, he published a work, Collectanea Sacra, full of material of Irish interest.

In 1630, Father Fleming was sent to be head of a new Franciscan college in Prague. This college had been set up by the Emperor, Ferdinand II to relieve the pressure of Irish Franciscan vocations at Louvain and Rome. Unfortunately, for this project and for Father Fleming, Saxon Protestant troops were on the march and they mounted an attack on Prague. In that situation, Catholics were everywhere in danger, especially Catholic priests. The Saxons had, as allies, the local Bohemians who had for centuries resisted Austrian rule. As a result, many Bohemians became dedicated Lutherans. It was while he was walking with another Franciscan that Patrick Fleming found himself surrounded by armed peasants who wasted no time in butchering both of the priests.

Patrick Fleming has always been regarded as a martyr for the faith. He has always been venerated by his illustrious Order. He merits equal honour from his own people not only for his devotion to the Faith, crowned by his martyrdom, but also for his monumental contribution to placing on record the achievements of Irish missionaries in Europe, and thus establishing the Golden Age of Ireland.

John Meagh, SJ   1639
31 May

John Meagh was a contemporary of Patrick Fleming, and indeed their careers were strikingly similar. Their deaths took place in the same locality and under almost identical conditions. The Cause for Canonisation of John Meagh was begun in 1904.

He was from Cork and like so many other Irishmen he fled to Europe to avoid the persecution of Catholics. Unlike so many others, however, he had no immediate idea of a vocation, although he was deeply concerned about what he could do for his people at home. He chose to live for a while in Naples and it was there that he received the inspiration to take up a vocation which was to end in martyrdom.

It is said that he turned to a book on the lives of saints to seek some guidance as to his future. The story which most held his attention was the life of Dymphna of Gheel. To be sure this story has always been one of the most powerful influences on the faithful and the cult of Dymphna has never been extinguished and is even growing at the present time, especially in the USA.

What it was precisely about Dymphna which finally decided John Meagh is not known. Perhaps it was the nature of her steadfast faith and martyrdom. Perhaps it was the truly miraculous effect her example had in changing indifference and even hostility towards the mentally afflicted into the enthusiastic devotion to their welfare which has been a feature of Gheel for centuries in memory of Dymphna, the Irish Princess, butchered by her incestuous father in a fit of madness.

Almost immediately, John Meagh presented himself to the Society of Jesus and was accepted as a novice. The Jesuits, like the Franciscans in the case of Patrick Fleming, had had to open a college near Prague, at Guttenberg, and John Meagh was soon in the centre of a military situation. This time Prague was under siege by Swedish Lutheran troops, again, in this case, aided by Protestant Bohemians.

The bitter feuds which lingered on in Europe between Catholics and Protestants were specially severe in this part of Europe. The Holy Roman Empire which adhered to the Catholic faith was finding that many of the peoples and states owing it allegiance were opting for a Protestant faith, mostly Lutheran, and religion became with increasing bitterness the excuse for continual warfare against the Empire. This was specially true at the time in Bohemia, with Prague as its capital. It was in these circumstances that the Jesuit College at Gutenberg was destroyed by Swedish Protestant troops and all the Jesuits took to flight. All of them escaped, except John Meagh who was martyred on the spot by local peasants.

Ralph Corby   1644
7 September

Born in Maynooth in Ireland, he was martyred with the English martyrs, and beatified by Pope Pius XI in 1929. His entire family, including his father and mother, his sisters and brothers all took religious vows. He himself became a Jesuit in Flanders and ministered to the faithful in Durham for twelve years till his arrest. It is said that Jesuits abroad were working to have him spared in return for the release of a Scottish colonel held prisoner in Germany. The arrangements however did not work out and sentence of death was passed on Corby and his fellow prisoner, John Duckett, who also was revealed as a priest. On a point of law, Corby claimed that, as he was born in Ireland, his trial was unconstitutional, but to no avail.

It is recorded that, in spite of elaborate precautions to destroy the bodies, the hand of John Duckett and pieces of the clothing of both of them were saved, although there seems to be no information as to where they are now.

Charles Mihan (Meehan)   1639–1679
12 August

Confusion has arisen over this martyr, due to uncertainty over his name, the name Mahony having often been used. It is now accepted that that name is incorrect. Possibly because of this confusion, precise records of his place of birth and early life are lacking. He was, apparently, already ministering to the people as a Franciscan in Ireland in 1672. He had to flee to the continent to avoid arrest and for some five years, studied in Franciscan establishments in Flanders, Germany and Rome. He set off to return to Ireland in 1678 but his ship was grounded in Wales during a storm. He was arrested just at the time when the Titus Oates story of an impending French invasion, inspired by Papists, was increasingly in circulation. As an Irishman, he was suspect, and when his trial revealed that he was a priest, he was condemned and executed.

He was declared Venerable by Pope Pius XI on 15 December 1929, and his cause still continues.

Catherine McAuley   1778–1841
10 November

The largest Order ever founded in the English-speaking world was launched in 1835 when the Holy See sanctioned the Order of Sisters of Mercy. Its foundress, Catherine McAuley died in 1841 by which time she had ten convents in Ireland and one in London. A century later, the Order had nearly 1,000 houses. The total has now grown to over 1,500.

This astonishing achievement was the work of an Irish woman, born in County Dublin, who spent the first part of her life resisting exceptional temptations to turn her back on her faith. By the age of seventeen, she had lost both parents. Her brother and sister went to live with Protestant relatives and lost their faith, although Catherine succeeded after some years in bringing her sister back. Catherine at first lived with Catholic relations but a drastic change in their fortunes forced Catherine also to enter the same home as her brother and sister, and there she remained for twenty years.

At that point, a remarkable change took place in her fortunes. She was invited by Protestant friends of her relatives, a childless couple, to enter their home to act as companion to the wife who was in poor health. Before long, this lady died and three years later the husband also passed away. Some measure of the power of Catherine's example can be gauged by the fact that both of them were received into the Catholic Church before they died. To Catherine's astonishment, she was named in the will as the sole beneficiary and found herself the mistress of a large property and £25,000.

From that time, in 1822, until her death, she devoted all her energy and resources to providing facilities of all kinds for the needs of the poor. Her first thoughts were given to education, and she sold her property and opened her first establishment, a residential home for girls and women, and in 1827 the first of the school of the Sisters of Mercy was in operation. She had a chapel and a chaplain, but had not intended to found an Order, believing that she could carry out her mission through a lay community.

Not surprisingly, pressures both from her own community and from the Archdiocese made her revise that view and the Order of Sisters of Mercy was the result. The attention of the Catholic world had been immediately drawn to this whole enterprise and the number of applicants for vocations was something of a phenomenon, especially in view of the diversity of work carried out by the Order. It is not generally known, for example, that of the thirty-eight nurses who formed Florence Nightingale's team in the Crimean War, no less than twenty were Sisters of Mercy. As this was only thirteen years after the death of Catherine, it indicates something of the strength and vitality of the movement she founded.

A tribute from Florence Nightingale to the work of the Sisters of Mercy in the Crimea is contained in a letter she sent to Mother Clare Moore, the leader of the group. The admiration she felt for the spiritual qualities which the Sisters displayed is evident in all she said. While her comments were addressed to those who actually served her, they were, in fact, an expression of the highest praise for the dedication which was already an essential part of the traditions of the Order, and this dedication came directly from the saintly example of its Foundress.

Catherine McAuley is one of those Servants of God whose sanctity was already widely acknowledged during her lifetime. It was, indeed, her own contemporaries who pressed from the beginning for the opening of her Cause. In fact, it was opened in 1953, backed by the prayers of the communities in over 1,500 houses of the Order, and countless students and others who have enjoyed the privilege of contact with the Sisters of Mercy. It is worth a comment that this Order, following the traditions of the Foundress, have always occupied a leading role in every aspect of social service.

Edmund Ignatius Rice 1762–1844
29 August

The Founder of the Christian Brothers and the Presentation Brothers, Rice was born at Callan, Co. Kilkenny, on 1 June 1762. He was the son of a prosperous farmer. His father's brother, a well-to-do merchant in Waterford, took him as a learner into his business which was to be Edmund's career. In 1785, he married, only to lose his wife four years later in a fatal hunting accident. This tragedy turned his thoughts towards a vocation to which he devoted much thought.

He lived during a particularly depressed time for Irish Catholics. He himself was one of the few affluent Catholics and Edmund had seen only too clearly in Waterford the poverty in which they lived. In his planning, it became more and more clear that education was the real key to opportunity and he decided to set up an organisation to provide this for poor Irish boys. So in 1803, with the encouragement both of the Pope and the Bishops, he started his first school in Waterford. Six years later, he formed the nucleus of his religious Order which was based on the Rule of the Presentation Sisters.

This did not prove the ideal basis for what he had in mind and he revised the Rule to follow that of another Order of Brothers, founded by St. John Baptist de la Salle. His new Order was then authorised in 1821, and he became the first Superior General of the Christian Brothers. By the time he died in 1844, there were over twenty Houses of the Order which is now world-wide with, in 1976, 344 Houses.

In discussing the Order he founded, it always seems necessary to clarify its separate existence. The work it does and the areas in which it is active have led to constant confusion with the De La Salle Brothers who are very frequently and wrongly called Christian Brothers. In fact, the real name of the De La Salle Brothers is Brothers of the Christian Schools. A second difference between them is that Edmund Rice's Order, the Christian Brothers, is quite definitely of Irish origin. The Brothers of the Christian Schools are a French Order, although they have had over the years a great many Irish vocations.

Both of these Orders are very active in Ireland, and are jointly responsible for a high proportion of the teaching of Irish boys both at primary and secondary level. They also, especially the Brothers of the Christian Schools were pioneers in the establishment of schools for delinquents. In various parts of the world, both Orders have also entered into University training as well as being a major source of the training of teachers for Catholic schools.

The Christian Brothers are quite famous in the USA for their University College of Iona in La Rochelle. This College is a leading centre of Irish studies in the USA and is constantly the venue of important Irish Cultural Conventions. Not far away, incidentally, is Manhattan College in New York City, conducted by the Brothers of the Christian Schools.

Edmund Ignatius Rice is one of those Servants of God whose devotion led to a flourishing Order, dedicated to a service of great value to the Church and to society. He is, in addition, almost unique in that he was the founder not of one but two Orders, for the Presentation Brothers, who now have 33 Houses, also claim him as their founder. He is widely venerated and his cause is proceeding.

Mary Aikenhead   1787–1858
19 January

Mary Aikenhead was the eldest of three daughters of a Cork doctor, a staunch Protestant. Ironically enough, it was her poor health which led to her being sent to live in the country in a Catholic home where, for six years, she experienced Catholicism in a manner which was to affect her own life. She returned to her own family, but her Catholic leanings persisted and when she was twelve she was secretly baptised into the Church. An astonishing event, two years later, was the last minute conversion of her father who died in 1801 without, apparently, ever knowing that Mary was already a Catholic.

Mary became increasingly involved in social work among the poor, and before long attracted the attention of Archbishop Murray of Dublin who had for long wanted to see an Order of Sisters of Charity formed in his Diocese. Mary had informed him that she would like to enter such an Order which, he told her, would be formed as soon as he could find a Reverend Mother. In due course, he sent for her and she came fully expecting to be offered the opportunity to enter.

In the event, what he told her was not what she expected. He asked her to become the Reverend Mother thus founding, perhaps for the only time, an Order with no nuns but only the head of the Community, before the Community was formed. Very quickly, she was joined by Alicia Walsh, and they were received as nuns by the Bishop. So began the Sisters of Charity whose work was dictated at the outset by a raging epidemic of cholera in Dublin. It was this first experience which led Mary Aikenhead to the conclusion that the major aim of the Order should be the provision of a hospital for the poor of Dublin, and her prayers were directed to that end.

The result, of course, has been one of the truly great institutions of Ireland, St. Vincent's Hospital in Dublin. Providentially, it happened that an early novice brought with her a dowry of £3,000. What was equally important was that her brother, a physician, offered his services without charge. Mary was thus able to purchase the site in Stephen's Green, Dublin, which was for so long associated with this famous hospital, and Dr. O'Ferrall became the first of its doctors.

While the Order is so closely connected with the care of the sick, it has been associated also with every activity concerned with suffering. The Sisters of Charity have from the beginning inspired active life among the unfortunate. It was these Sisters who were to the fore in helping the convicts of Australia to adjust to a life which appeared to be devoid of all hope, during and after their imprisonment.

A remarkable miracle, clearly due to her intercession, is widely known to many people still alive. It was brought about by Father John Sullivan, the Irish Jesuit who is himself one of the Irish Causes under investigation. He applied a relic of Mary Aikenhead to a woman suffering from an incurable disease, and an immediate cure resulted.

For more than twenty-five years until her death, Mary Aikenhead was seriously disabled by spinal trouble, yet she continued to inspire her followers. It is an extraordinary fact that she was unable to see or visit establishments which she herself founded in Ireland. Among those which are now directed by her Order are hospitals and schools, including a secondary school in California, one of the biggest in the USA. Throughout the world, the activities of the Sisters of Charity reflect the correct interpretation of their title, and of the truly charitable intentions of their foundress whose cause was initiated by a Decree of Benedict XV in 1921. Finally, Mary Aikenhead was the first Irish woman to be honoured by the issue of a commemorative stamp on the centenary of her death, a unique tribute by the nation who owed her so much.

Dom Columba Marmion, OSB   1858–1923
30 January

Joseph Columba Marmion was born in Dublin in 1858, the youngest of nine children of a Dublin merchant and a French mother, the daughter of the French Consul in Dublin. After an education at the Jesuit College, Belvedere, in Dublin, Holy Cross Seminary, Clonliffe, the Irish College and the College of Propaganda in Rome, he was ordained in 1881 for the Dublin Diocese. Later he entered the Benedictine Abbey at Maredsous, Belgium, and in 1899 he was made Prior of the Abbey of Mont César at Louvain. He was also a Professor in the University of Louvain. Because of his writing and the wide prestige he acquired for his inspiring Retreats, he became something of an international figure.

It was a tribute to his fame that he was invited to act as spiritual adviser to the Anglican community at Caldy while they were considering a mass conversion to the Catholic Church. Their subsequent decision to enter the Church, therefore, must be considered as being due, at least in part, to the influence of Dom Columba, as he was now known in the Benedictine Order.

When the First World War broke out, he was Abbot of Maredsous. He led his community out of Belgium and reached Ireland. It is due to him, primarily, that his Order was re-established in his native land and, indeed, Glenstall Abbey is one of the results and is, understandably, under his patronage. Another Benedictine Abbey in the USA is not only under his patronage, but bears his name. This is Marmion Abbey in Aurora, Illinois.

When he returned to Maredsous, he was to prove that he was very much an Irishman. He suffered agonies of sorrow for the sufferings of Ireland at this time. To add to the violence of armed conflicts, the activities of Black and Tans, the pogroms against Catholics in Northern Ireland, there was, perhaps most distressing of all to Dom Columba, the hostility of Irishmen against Irishmen. It was at this time that the Irish Bishops appealed to Cardinal Mercier to intercede for the Irish people, and his closest adviser was Dom Columba. The Cardinal's appeal for Ireland is now famous, not least because he recalled what his own country owed to Irish missionaries of the past. He quoted many of them by name and stressed the extent of the veneration they inspired among his own countrymen.

Dom Columba is, of course, best known as a great teacher and scholar whose books are available in ten languages. His cause was officially opened in 1954, but like many other Servants of God his cult began, both in Belgium and in Ireland, from the moment of his death. His body lies in the Abbey of Maredsous.

Matthew Talbot   1856–1925
7 June

Matthew Talbot died in 1925 and his cause is being studied in Rome. Few Irishmen have caught the imagination of his people as he has done. It happens also that his much heralded escape from alcoholism coincides with the modern concern about this social problem. Most of all, however, it is his very lowly circumstances which have made him something of a symbol of the ordinary people of the working classes of Dublin. This same feature has contributed to the widespread interest in him far outside Ireland. His life was dreary, his education was almost nil, his material prospects negligible. He might have died in the same obscurity had the accident of his death in hospital after collapse in the street not revealed the chains around his body. Inevitably, curiosity was aroused and his very obscurity increased the mystery and the interest in his life. Within a year, his story was circulating in at least a dozen languages. His cult was immediate and has grown to proportions seldom equalled. Many people are still alive who recall the excitement caused by his death. His canonisation is widely expected at all levels of society. If and when it does come about, he is already elected by many of his devoted followers to be the hope and inspiration of all problem drinkers whose desperate need for hope and inspiration exceeds that of most other sections of mankind.

John Sullivan, SJ   1861–1933
19 February

John Sullivan, S J, died in 1933 and his cause is now with the Sacred Congregation for the Causes of Saints. He was born in 1861, the son of a Protestant, a Lord Chancellor and a baronet. Father Sullivan had the classic upbringing of the old Protestant Ascendancy, Portora Royal and Trinity College, Dublin. He was himself a lawyer with brilliant prospects. In 1901, he astonished and no doubt shocked his Irish Protestant friends when he entered the Jesuit Order. He lived for thirty-two years in comparative obscurity, for he was mostly employed teaching at Clongowes. Even so, his extraordinary virtue and sanctity became increasingly known in his own lifetime, and when he died his cult started immediately. In 1960, in order to facilitate the cause, his body was exhumed and transferred from Clongowes to St. Francis Xavier's Jesuit Church in Dublin. The occasion led to a remarkable demonstration of devotion along the entire route.

Edel Mary Quinn   1907–1944
12 May

Edel Mary Quinn died in 1944 and her cause is now under way. Quite early in her life, she became involved in the Legion of Mary which she left for a time to become a Poor Clare. She underwent almost two years of treatment for tuberculosis and returned to her work with the Legion of Mary which was to fill her life. For seven years, till she died at the age of thirty-seven, she led the pioneer work of the Legion in Africa. Her old illness was always with her and she had two more years in hospital. Among others with whom she worked was Mother Kevin who had a constant anxiety in restraining the enthusiasm of her delicate assistant. She died in Nairobi and is buried there. The Bishop there is on record as saying that her very brief presence there changed for ever the atmosphere of his entire diocese.

CHAPTER VII

Important Irish Feast Days

One of the most popular books on Irish sanctity is the *Book of Irish Saints* by Eoin Neeson, published in Ireland in 1967. It contains some 1,400 names. The author stresses in the Introduction that this is only a fraction of the total, and that many Saints have left behind them no more than their names. In other words, the 1,400 names he does quote represent strict selection, a selection which allows for something like three or four names for every day of the year. The list which follows here is still more selective. It contains the names of all those who are described or referred to throughout this book, and those whose cults seem to be most enduring. It does not, of course, contain any of the names on the List of Irish Martyrs except St. Oliver Plunkett.

In this way, only those are included who could be said to represent clearly all those elements that this book has tried to stress. Much has been said about the traditional saints. It has seemed important to include only those whose cult is strongly established. It was equally important to identify the saint with the local area which is the centre of the cult, as clearly as the evidence allowed. This is relevant both inside and outside Ireland in a work of this kind.

Given the long period of time covered by the lives of these saints, it is inevitable that the exact location of their area of influence is not always easy to define as the ancient names may no longer exist. In the case of Irish missions in Europe in the early centuries, the modern geographical divisions are, of course, very different. Petty kingdoms have been absorbed into great nations and it is not always easy to define exactly where the area of activity of a particular saint is to be found on a modern map.

In the case of Ireland itself, the name of a locality in the early centuries may be totally lost, even when it actually bore the name of the saint himself. A major example is the City of Limerick, a name which was used by the Vikings, in place of the old Gaelic name taken from the patron, Munchin Luimnich.

The choice of saints listed below has been as selective as is possible under all the circumstances. They are intended to illustrate all the aspects of Irish sanctity which have been discussed under the various headings in this book. The canonised saints, of course, are included. So are those Irish Causes actually in progress as well as those who have received official recognition from various Popes in the past. The rest are all traditional saints, and all can reasonably be said to be the objects of continuing cults. Not all of them are well known to all Irish people. It can, however, be said that all of them have their devotees somewhere. In compiling such a list it could never be said that all those names have been included which merit inclusion. Equally, it can reasonably be said that no name is quoted here which does not merit inclusion.

It should be said again at this stage that there is academic discussion as to whether all those claimed as Irish are genuine. In this book and in this chapter, it is accepted that if the traditional cult is linked also with the tradition that the Saint is Irish, the tradition is accepted in its entirety. Equally such cases as Duns Scotus, considered by many to belong among Irish causes, does not figure in this book. This is because in those areas of Europe where he is venerated, there is no Irish tradition.

JANUARY

1. **Fanchea (Fainche)** of Rossory, Fermanagh   c. 520
   One of the early nuns, specially recorded in Irish history for having persuaded her brother, Enda, to become a monk. He is generally regarded as the father of Irish monasticism (v. Enda of Aran – 21 March).

2. **Munchin (Munchin Luimnich)** of Limerick   7th century
   The city of Limerick grew out of his establishment at Inis Ibhton on the Shannon, and derived its Gaelic name Luimnich from him. He is also said to have founded the school at Mungret.

7. **Kentigerna** of Loch Lomand, Scotland   c. 733
   She is associated in the Scottish Mission with her brother, Comghan (v. 13 October) and her son Fillan (v. 9 January).

8. **Erhart** (Albert) of Ratisbon   c. 686
   (v. p. 74).

9. **Fillan (Foillan)** of Strathfillan, Scotland   8th century

History records that Robert Bruce put his hopes of victory at Bannockburn into the hands of St. Fillan. It is said that he brought a relic of the Saint into battle having passed most of the night praying for his intercession. Not surprisingly, the Scots victory at Bannockburn did much to revive and perpetuate the cult of St. Fillan.

14. **Kentigern (Mungo) of Glasgow** c. 603
This is the saint who figures on the coat of arms of Glasgow. He was probably Irish since his nickname Mungo is compounded with the prefix "Mo", a purely Irish custom. He revived the traditions of Ninian in Strathclyde and restored his church in Glasgow. His mother, Thenog, gave her name to St. Enoch's Square and Railway Station in that city.

15. **Ita (Mida) of Killeedy, Co. Limerick** 570
Next to Brigid, the most famous of Irish women saints. She is known as the Brigid of Munster. She acted as foster mother to many eminent Irish Saints, notably Brendan of Clonfert (the Navigator). (v. p. 49)

16. **Fursa of Peronne,** France (v. p. 37) 649

18. **Ninidh** of Lough Erne 6th century
One of the Twelve Apostles of Ireland (v. Finian, 12 December). The tradition is that Brigid sent for him to administer the Last Sacraments to her.

18. **Desle (Dicuil) of Lure, France** 625
Founder of the great French Abbey and city of Lure in Northern France. The Abbots of this monastery were made Princes of the Holy Roman Empire more than 1,000 yyears later. He was one of the companions of Columban, and remained behind him when he left France. His cult is very strong around Lure.

19. **Mary Aikenhead** 1787–1858
(v. p. 100).

19 **Blaithmac of Iona** c. 825
His martyrdom led the German Benedictine Strabo to write his biography. It seems he was temporarily in charge of Iona when it was raided by Vikings. According to the tradition, he foretold the raid and buried the shrine containing the relics of Columba. The Vikings slaughtered the whole community. Blaithmac was spared till the last, and promised immunity if

he handed over the relics. He refused and was butchered on the steps of the altar. The relics were placed in Dunkeld in 849.

20. **Fechin of Fore,** Co. Westmeath   665
Listed in Scottish calendars under the name of Vigean, he gave his name to Ecclefechin and St. Vigean's near Arbroath. His monastery became famous because of the well he is reputed to have created out of a rock. His Abbey at Cong is celebrated because of the Cross of Cong, one of the great treasures of Ireland, now in the National Museum in Dublin.

20. **Molacca (Molagga)** of Fermoy, Co. Cork   7th century
Much venerated in N. Cork, round the area of his foundation at Fermoy. He is also associated with Balbriggan, Dublin.

21. **Maolcalain (Malcallan)** of Waulsort, Belgium   c. 978
Malcallan was one of a group who left Ireland during the Viking terror, and joined the Irish Abbey at Peronne. Not far away, he founded the Abbey of St. Michael at Thierache. He set up another at Waulsort in Belgium. In 946, the Emperor Otto I issued a charter which stipulated that this should be governed by an Irish Abbot so long as one was available within the community.

24. **Guasacht of Granard,** Co. Longford   5th century
It is said that Patrick went to see his former master, Miluic, under whom he worked as a slave. Miluic set fire to his house and perished in the flames rather than meet his former slave. His son, Guasacht, and his daughters, the two Emers (v. 11 December) became Christians, and Guasacht was the first Bishop of Granard, Co. Longford.

26. **Conan of the Isle of Man**   649
Venerated in the Isle of Man as the first Bishop of Sodor.

29. **Dallan Forghaill** of Inniskeel, Co. Donegal   c. 598
Chief Bard of Ireland, he wrote a eulogy of Columba, the "Amra Colmcille" after Columba had saved the Bardic Order at the Convention of Drumceat (v. Columba, p. 26). Dallan Forghaill is the most famous poet-saint of Ireland and is venerated as a martyr, having been savagely done to death by pagan sea pirates at his island monastery at Inniskeel.

30. **Eusebius of Mount St. Victor,** Switzerland   884
He lived a life of solitude on Mount St. Victor, near the city

of St. Gall (v. Gall p. 46). The Emperor erected an Irish monastery for him on the Mount and a hospice for Irish pilgrims. He is venerated as a martyr since he was beaten to death by peasants whom he had rebuked for their sins.

30. **Dom Columba Marmion**   1858–1923
(v. p. 102).

31. **Aidan of Ferns,** Co. Wexford   626
Trained at St. David's Abbey at Menevia, Wales. It is a tradition that St. David died in the arms of Aidan. It is also a Welsh tradition that he succeeded St. David as Abbot. On the strength of that, a claim was later made from Wales to establish Welsh jurisdiction over Ferns, since it was claimed it was founded by a Welsh Abbot, i.e. Aidan.

31. **Adamnan of Coldingham,** Scotland   680
(v. p. 57).

FEBRUARY

1. **Brigid of Kildare**   525
(v. p. 20).

2. **Columban of Ghent, Belgium**   959
He was probably an Abbot in Ireland who led his community to Belgium following constant Viking raids. He acquired a wide reputation for sanctity, as he lived out his life in a cell in the cemetery of St. Bavo's Church in Ghent. He is now buried in the Cathedral and is one of the patrons of Belgium.

3. **Ives of St. Ives,** Cornwall   5th century
An Irish nun who came to Cornwall and built her cell near the mouth of the Hayle river. The area is now called after her.

5. **Indract of Glastonbury**   8th century
Indract and his sister, Dominica (Drusa) were returning to Ireland after a pilgrimage to Rome when they were martyred near Glastonbury and a strong cult arose immediately. They were enshrined in the Abbey at Glastonbury and venerated as martyrs.

5. **Fingen of Metz**   c. 1005
He acquired a reputation for restoring old abbeys and one of them, St. Symphorien's, was given over to him and an Irish community. Pope John XVII issued a Charter which declared

109

that only Irish monks would administer the Abbey. Fingen's relics lie in St. Clement's Church in Metz.

6. **Mel of Longford,** Co. Longford   c. 488
Traditionally said to have professed Brigid as a nun. One of the very early Irish Bishops, his memory is strongly venerated in Longford, where the Cathedral bears his name.

7. **Tressan of Avenay,** Rheims, France   6th century
(v. p. 73).

9. **Marianus Scotus of Ratisbon,** Germany   1088
(v. p. 45).

9. **Alto of Altomunster,** Bavaria   c. 760
King Pepin heard of the sanctity of this Irish monk and founded for him a monastery which took his name and became famous as Altomunster. In the year 1000, according to tradition, he appeared to the King of Bavaria and asked him to restore the Abbey, which he did. It still survives and has been a Brigittine convent for five centuries.

11. **Gobnait of Ballyvourney,** Co. Cork   6th century
(v. p. 72).

12. **Sedulius (Seadhal)**   5th century
(v. p. 71).

17. **Fintan of Clonenagh,** Co. Laois   603
Famous for the severity of his rule, regarded by many as too severe. It is said that he was a discipline of St. David of Wales, whose aversion to alcohol earned him the name of "The Waterman". Fintan's rule strongly reflected the same aversion.

18. **Colman of Lindisfarne**   676
(v. p. 34).

19. **John Sullivan SJ** (v. p. 104)   1861–1933

20. **Colchu (Colgu) of Clonmacnoise**   c. 796
Noted for the influence he exerted on the Imperial schools in France, through his students. Apart from his Irish students, it has been established that Alcuin, the most famous English scholar in Europe at the time studied under Colchu.

MARCH

1. **Marnoc of Kilmarnock,** Scotland   7th century
A disciple of St. Columba of Iona (v. p. 26), he gave his name

to Kilmarnock. Some historians think he is the same person as St. Marnanus of Annandale, also celebrated today.

1. **Marnanus of Annandale,** Scotland   620
   One of the Apostles of Northumbria, he is much venerated in the Border country of Scotland.

5. **Ciaran (Kieran) of Saigher,** Co. Offaly   5th century
   (v. p. 17). One of the Twelve Apostles of Ireland (v. Finian, 12 December).

6. **Fridolin of Sackingen,** Switzerland   6th century
   (v. p. 47).

8. **Senan of Inis Cathaigh** (Scattery Island)   544
   He established both a school and a bishopric on the island. The Cloghan Oir or Golden Bell of St. Senan is in the National Museum in Dublin. One of the best preserved round towers is still in existence on the island.

10. **Attalas of Bobbio**   7th century
    One of St. Columban's companions till that great Abbot died. Attalas succeeded him as Abbot and died at Bobbio.

10. **Hymelin of Vissenacken**   8th century
    Said to have been the brother of St. Rumold of Malines (v. 3 July). His shrine at Vissenacken, Belgium, is a noted centre for pilgrims.

11. **Aengus the Culdee**   842
    Aengus spent his life at Clonenagh Abbey. He was the originator of the "Ceile De (Culdee)" movement in monasticism, otherwise referred to as the "Companion of God" movement, the name given to him by his devotees. He was probably the first to compile a list of Irish saints, "The Martyrology of Tallaght", in collaboration with St. Maelruin of Tallaght (v. 7 July).

16. **Abban of Kill Abban, Leinster**   5th century
    Alleged to have been the nephew of St. Ibar (v. p. 16) and contemporary of St. Patrick. It was he who established the convent for St. Gobnait of Ballyvourney (v. p. 72).

17. **St. Patrick, Apostle of Ireland**   387–465
    (v. p. 18).

18. **Frigidian (Fridian) of Lucca,** Italy   588
    (v. p. 75).

19. **Lactan of Freshford,** Co. Kilkenny   634–672
Born near Cork, and educated by Comgall of Bangor (v. 10 May) who instructed him to found his Abbey at Freshford. He is credited with many miracles and with cures of paralytics and the mentally ill.

20. **Cuthbert of Durham**   687
Possibly the most venerated of all the saints in England. His exact nationality is not clear and the Venerable Bede did not specify it in his writings. There is strong evidence that he was Irish, that his real name was Mulloche, and that he was the grandson of Muircertagh, High King of Ireland. The little seashells found only in his island retreat in the Farne Islands are traditionally known as St. Cuthbert's Beads, and are said to have been made by him.

20. **Clement of the Paris Schools**   c. 826
One of the most famous of the Irish scholars at the Court of the Carolovingian Emperors. He was head of the Paris Schools after the Englishman, Alcuin.

21. **Enda of Aran**   c. 535
Originally a warrior, he embraced the monastic life on the advice of his sister, St. Fanchea (v. 1 January) after the death of his intended bride. It is generally accepted that he set the standard for Irish monasticism by the model he established in Aran.

22. **Darerca, Sister of St. Patrick**   5th century
Little is known of her except that she is alleged to have been the mother of other saints in Ireland.

24. **Caimin of Lough Derg**   654
His austere life on Lough Derg and miracles attributed to him, attracted many disciples. He is said to have later founded a monastery on "The Island of the Seven Churches". His manuscript "The Psalter of St. Caimin" still exists. He may be the same St. Caimin listed for 25 March who is also associated with Lough Derg. He is credited with authorship of the Commentary on the Hebrew Text of the Psalms.

24. **Donard of Maghera,** Co. Down   506
Lived as a hermit on the mountain to which he gave his name, Slieve Donard.

24. **MacCartan of Clogher,** Co. Monaghan   5th century
Appointed by St. Patrick as first Bishop of Clogher in 454.

This is one of the oldest Irish bishoprics still in existence. It is said that St. Brigid was present at its founding. The Cloch-Oir or Golden Stone from which Clogher takes its name is still preserved at Clogher.

25. **Caimin of Inniscaltra** 653
Founded his monastery on Lough Derg. Possibly the same person as the Saint Caimin listed yesterday (v. 24 March).

26. **Sinell of Killeagh,** Leinster 5th century
An early Roman convert of St. Patrick. His Abbey at Killeagh survived until the Reformation. The organ and stained glass windows were removed and installed in the Protestant Church at Maynooth.

27. **Gelasius, Archbishop of Armagh** 1174
Became Archbishop in 1137 when St. Malachy resigned (v. p. 57). Gelasius had the sad task of dealing with the events before and after the Norman invasion and has long been venerated as a saint. He was succeeded by Conchobar MacConaille, venerated under the name of St. Concord in the Archdiocese of Chambéry, France. (v. p. 76).

30. **Patto of Verden,** Germany 8th century
He was established as Abbot of the Irish monastery at Anabaric and later as Bishop of Verden. Many miracles have been attributed to him and his body was exhumed in 1630. There seems to be no record of the result of this, which is common in papal investigations of sanctity.

30. **Riaghail of Rigmond** (St. Andrews), Scotland 6th century
He was also known as Regulus or Rule. A leading Scottish authority on Celtic history considers that the story of the origin of St. Andrews has confused this Regulus with a mythical Greek of the same name who is supposed to have brought relics of St. Andrew the Apostle to Rigmond and thus founded St. Andrews. In fact, the relics were acquired by a Pictish King on 736 and he founded the city. The Abbot at the time was the Irish Tuathal.

APRIL

1. **Celsus (Ceallach) of Armagh** 1129
Celsus was a lay hereditary Abbot of Armagh, but made up his mind to end the long-standing scandal of lay control of

important Church appointments. He took Holy Orders, became the Bishop of Armagh and played a major role in restoring Armagh as the primatial See. As his death approached, in 1129, he sent his crozier to St. Malachy and named him as his successor.

1. **Caidoc and Fricor** of Centule, France   7th century
   These were the Irish monks who converted the French nobleman, Riquier, who founded the Abbey of Centule (now St. Riquier) about 625. This Abbey followed the Rule of St. Columbanus. Caidoc and Fricor were for long venerated at St. Riquier.

2. **Bronach of Kilbroney,** Co. Down   6th century
   St. Bronach's Bell is the subject of a well-known legend. In 1885, a storm brought down an oak tree in the Killbroney neighbourhood and in the branches was found a 6th century bell. For many years ,the inhabitants had heard a bell ringing and attributed to it a supernatural origin. In fact it seems to have been hidden to prevent it being removed at the Reformation. It is now used in the Parish Church of Rostrevor, Co. Down.

5. **Becan (Beggan) of Kilbeggan,** Co. Meath   6th century
   Founded Kilbeggan, called after him, and this became an important Cistercian Abbey.

6. **Berchan of Inishmore,** Galway
   Said to have been at one time Bishop of Kirkwall in the Orkneys. He was known traditionally as the Fear da Leithe, the Man of Two Places.

7. **Brenach (Bryynach) of Carn-Engyle,** Wales   5th century
   Believed to be the first Irish saint to spend his priestly life in Wales. The tradition is that he had constant communication with angels, and the mountain on which he had his retreat was called Car-Engyle, Mountain of the Angels.

8. **Beoadh (Beatus) of Ardcarne, Co. Roscommon**   6th century
   His name was Aodh to which was added the prefix *bo*. He was made Bishop of Ardcarne, Co. Roscommon. The Bell of St. Beoadh was a famous object of veneration in Connaught. Its present whereabouts are unknown, and it may have been lost at the Reformation.

10. **Paternus of Abdinghof,** Germany   1058
    A recluse who lived in a cell near the monastery. He openly

rebuked the people of Paderborn, the nearby town, for their evil lives and finally foretold that fire would destroy it within thirty days. In fact, fire did break out in several places destroying the town and the cell of Paternus who perished in the flames. A strong cult of Paternus arose immediately, centred round the mat on which he prayed, which miraculously escaped the flames and became an object of veneration.

12. **Ailill of Cologne,** Germany   1042
Ailill was known as Elias. He came from Co. Monaghan about 1020, and was elected Abbot of St. Martin's which had been declared an Irish Abbey. While he was there, a second Abbey in Cologne. St. Pantaleon's was also reserved for the Irish.

12. **Edel Mary Quinn**   1907–1944
(v. p. 104).

12. **Erkembodon of St. Omer,** France   734
Abbot and Bishop of St. Omer. So many miracles occurred at his shrine that pilgrims came in great numbers, and their offerings were such that a few years after his death, it was possible to build a Cathedral in his honour.

14. **Tassach of Raholp,** Co. Down   c. 490
Placed by St. Patrick as first Bishop of Raholp, he is said to have administered the Last Sacraments to St. Patrick. He was famous for his skill in making ecclesiastical objects. It seems that confusion may have arisen between him and St. Assic of Elphin (v. 27 April) who had the same skills and clearly bore a very similar name, and the same year of death is quoted in both cases.

15. **Ruadhan of Lorrha,** Co. Tipperary   c. 584
One of the Twelve Apostles of Ireland (v. Finian of Clonard, 12 December). The famous Stowe Missal was produced at Lorrha. The most famous legend concerning St. Ruadhan is the Cursing of Tara. According to this, the King of Connaught fled for sanctuary to Lorrha to escape the wrath of the High King whose emissary he had allegedly executed. The High King invaded Lorrha and dragged his victim out. Ruadhan assembled a group of saints of Ireland before the seat of the High King of Tara and laid a solemn curse on it for the violation of the laws of sanctuary, due by tradition to the monasteries.

18. **Cogitosus of Kildare**   7th century
Best known for his Life of St. Brigid, a valuable guide to the

great monastic settlement at Kildare. The original is in the Dominican Convent at Eichstadt in Bavaria.

18. **Deicola (Dicuil)** 7th century
Founder of the Abbey at Bosham, Sussex. He came there from St. Fursa's Abbey at Burghcastle in East Anglia (v. p. 37).

18. **Laiserian (Molaise) of Leighlin** 639
Nephew of St. Blane of Dunblane (v. 10 August), he was the founder of the Abbey of Leighlin and first Bishop. Later, he was Papal Legate to Ireland and strongly supported the Roman tradition against the Irish over the date of Easter.

21. **Maelrubba of Applecross,** Scotland 642–722
Maelrubba caused a great revival of the Celtic Church from his island settlement. His name can be traced in place-names all over the Western Highlands, notably in Loche Maree. Like many other Irish Saints in Scotland, he was specially invoked for the cure of insanity.

23. **Ibar (Ibhar) of Beggery Island,** Co. Wexford c. 490
(v. p. 16).

25. **Macaille of Croghan,** Co. Offaly c. 489
A disciple of St. Mel of Longford, he became the first Bishop of Croghan. He took part with St. Mel in receiving Brigid as a nun. There is a tradition that St. Mel in error used the service for consecration of a Bishop, and that Macaille protested very strongly. St. Mel refused to give way and said it was all the Will of God.

27. **Assicus (Assic) of Elphin,** Co. Mayo c. 490
First Bishop of Elphin, one of the ancient Bishoprics set up by St. Patrick in 450 and still surviving. The confusion between him and St. Tassach (v. 14 April) suggests that they may be the same person. They were both skilled metal-workers, their names are very similar and they died in the same year.

28. **Croman of Roscrea,** Co. Tipperary 665
Founder of the monastery at Roscrea. He is locally the object of long-standing veneration.

MAY

2. **Germanus of the Isle of Man** c. 460
The tradition is that this Irish colonist in Britain met St.

Germanus of Auxerre during his visit to Britain, became a Christian and adopted the name of Germanus. He was a Bishop with St. Patrick in Ireland and is alleged to have worked in Wales, Spain, Gaul and the Isle of Man of which he is held by some to be the Apostle. He was martyred in Normandy.

2. **Ultan of Fosses,** France   c. 686
A brother of the more famous St. Fursa of Peronne (v. p. 37), he was with him in his Abbey at Burghcastle in East Anglia and later in his Abbey at St. Quentin, France. He was later Abbot of Fursa's Abbey at Peronne. He was buried in the Abbey of Fosses, France, erected by another brother, St. Foillan.

3. **Conleth of Kildare**   519
When St. Brigid set up her two communities, one for men, the other for women, she invited St. Conleth to become the Bishop. This Bishopric is still in existence and is officially quoted in the *Annuario Pontificio,* the Vatican Yearbook, as being founded in 519.

5. **Diuma of Peterborough,** England   658
He was the first Bishop of Mercia. His monastery was dedicated to St. Peter. In due course, it became the modern city of Peterborough.

8. **Gibrian of St. Gibrian,** France   6th century
Gibrian laboured in the Diocese of Rheims and around his tomb has grown the town of St. Gibrian. His cult is based on numerous miracles, especially the restoration of sight, due to his intercession. He is buried in the Basilica of St. Remigius at Rheims.

9. **Beatus of Beatenburg,** Switzerland   9th century
His retreat at Lake Thun, Switzerland, is now the town of Beatenburg. He may be the same St. Beatus who, as Abbot of the Abbey at Honau on the Rhine, received from Charlemagne in 810 a Charter confirming that Honau was to be administered in perpetuity by Irish monks.

10. **Cattaldo (Cathal) of Taranto**   7th century
(v. p. 48).

10. **Congall of Bangor,** Co. Down   516–603
One of the famous founding Saints of Ireland. He was an Irish Pict and played an important part in obtaining for St. Columba

117

and St. Moluag permission from the Pictish King Brude to preach the Faith in Scotland. Congall founded the great School at Bangor, which trained some of the most eminent of the Irish missioners, Columbanus (v. p. 35), Gall (v. p. 46), Moluag (v. p. 30), Malachy (v. p. 57) and many others. St. Bernard of Clairvaux commented at great length on the importance in the early Church of this School. The literary treasure, "The Antiphonary of Bangor" which contains the oldest Eucharistic hymn "Sancti Venite" is in the Ambrosian Library in Milan.

11. **Cathan of Kilcathan,** Isle of Bute, Scotland   6th century
Uncle of St. Blane (v. 10 August), he was a Bishop in Bute. He is buried at Tamlacht, Co. Derry.

11. **Lua of Killaloe**   7th century
The ancient town of Killaloe is named after Lua. His sanctuary on Friar's Island in Co. Tipperary has been a place of pilgrimage well into the twentieth century. The famous legend of the horse's hoof-prints in the rock on the island tells of St. Patrick himself having been forced to leap from the shore to escape from hostile pagans and the hoof prints are a permanent record of the incident.

13. **Abban of Abingdon,** Berkshire, England   2nd century
(v. p. 15).

14. **Carthage Mochuda of Lismore,** Co. Waterford   637
Founded Lismore in 635 and it became immediately one of the most richly endowed and frequented of the monastic Schools of Ireland. A famous student there was St. Cathal (Cattaldo), Bishop of Taranto, Italy (v. p. 48). The Lismore Crozier is a treasured item of Irish art now in the National Museum in Dublin.

15. **Dymphna of Gheel,** Belgium   7th century
(v. p. 41).

16. **Brendan (The Navigator)** of Clonfert, Co. Galway   486–578
(v. p. 49).

17. **Mailduff of Malmesbury**   c. 673
Founder and titular Saint of the famous English Abbey of Malmesbury. His most famous student was the Anglo-Saxon scholar, Aldhelm.

18. **Conval of Strathclyde,** Scotland   6th century
Archdeacon to St. Kentigern of Glasgow (v 14 January). He
was active in the whole Strathclyde area south of Glasgow,
especially in the present county of Renfrewshire. The efforts
of extreme Reformers to eradicate devotion to old saints,
were especially intense in Conval's case. It is therefore quite
remarkable how his memory has survived to the extent that
there is a church dedicated to him at Pollokshaws, right in
the city of Glasgow.

21. **Sillao of Lucca,** Italy   1100
(v. p. 55).

30. **Maugille of Monstrelet,** France   c. 685
A companion of St. Fursa of Peronne (v. p. 37), he settled
after Fursa's death at Monstrelet where a strong cult has developed in his memory. Many miracles have been attributed
to his intercession.

31. **John Meagh, S J**   1639
(v. p. 95).

JUNE

1. **Ronan of Quimper,** Brittany   7th century
He is an important saint in the traditions of Brittany and in
the area round Laon. Several towns are called after him. There
is a long standing custom among the faithful to make a pro-
cessional pilgrimage every six years, along the traditional ten
mile route followed by Ronan in his Mission.

2. **Algise of St. Algise,** France   c. 686
Another of the companions of St. Fursa (v. p. 37). He spread
the gospel round Arras and the town of St. Algise is named in
his memory.

3. **Kevin of Glendalough**   618
Founder of the "City of Glendalough", probably the best-
preserved of the great monastic foundations of Ireland. Its
most famous Abbot in later times was St. Laurence O'Toole
(v. p. 61) one of the canonised Saints of Ireland. The devotion
to St. Kevin has never died and as late as 1980 large pilgrimages were made to the Abbey. The name Kevin is very popular
as a Christian name and is becoming more so at this time.

4. **Breaca (Breague)**   5th century
A well-known saint in Cornwall. He went there with several

119

companions about the year 460 and was martyred there on the river Hoyle.

4. **Concord (Conchobar MacConaille) of Chambéry,** France
    (v. p. 76).   1120–1176

5. **Eoban of Utrecht,** Germany   755
    Appointed Bishop of Utrecht by St. Boniface, the English
    Apostle of Germany, and martyred along with him at Dok-
    kum in Friesland.

5. **Adaler**   755
    Another Irish companion of Boniface, was martyred with him.

6. **Jarlath of Tuam**   c. 530
    Said to have been told by St. Brendan of Clonfert (v. p. 50)
    to drive his chariot till a wheel broke and build his Abbey
    there. A wheel broke at Tuam, Co. Galway when he set up
    his School in 520. Tuam is now one of the four Archbishop-
    rics of Ireland and the episcopal ring bears an engraving of
    the broken wheel. In 1979, a broken wheel was carried in pro-
    cession to Pope John Paul II when he visited Galway.

7. **Colman of Dromore,** Co. Down   c. 550
    First Bishop of Dromore, he is the titular saint of at least one
    church in Scotland, Inis Mo-Cholmaig, and Llangolman in
    Wales.

7. **Matthew Talbot**   1856–1925
    (v. p. 103)

9. **Columba (Colm, Colmcille) of Iona**   521–597
    (v. p. 26).

12. **Christian O'Morgair** of Clogher   1139
    Bishop of Clogher, he was the brother of St. Malachy (v. p. 57).
    His sanctity was specially commented on by St. Bernard
    of Clairvaux in his biography of St. Malachy.

16. **Berthold of Chaumont,** France   6th century
    (v. p. 74).

16. **Cettin (Cethach) of Oran**   5th century
    Consecrated as Auxiliary Bishop to assist St. Patrick. His
    shrine at Oran was a centre of pilgrimages for thirteen cen-
    turies.

17. **Moling of Ferns,** Co. Wexford   c. 697
    Founded Teach Moling (The House of Moling) which he left

when he succeeded Aidan as Bishop of Ferns (v. 31 January). It is said that he produced more Gaelic poems than any other Saint except St. Columba.

25. **Moloag of Lismore,** Scotland   530–592
(v. p. 30).

30. **Gobain of St. Gobain,** France   c. 670
Another of the companions of St. Fursa of Peronne (v. p. 37). He is one of the Irish Saints noted by the Venerable Bede. He was martyred on the spot which now bears his name. St. Gobain.

JULY

1. **Oliver Plunkett, Archbishop of Armagh**   1625–1681
(v. p. 67).

3. **Rumold of Malines,** Belgium   c. 775
The Cathedral of Malines is dedicated to him. He is the object of great veneration and his feast day is a major event there. He was martyred near there and lies in an elaborate golden shrine over the high altar in the Cathedral.

3. **Sunnifa of Norway**   10th century
Referred to by several authorities as an Irish nun who was shipwrecked in Norway and set up a convent with her companions. There is no information about her in Ireland.

4. **John Cornelius, Patrick Salmon, John Carey**   1594
(v. p. 93).

5. **Modwena of Polsworth, Warwickshire**   9th century
The Anglo-Saxon King Ethelwolfe brought Modwena to England after she cured his son of a supposedly incurable disease. He established two Abbeys for her and sent his daughter to her as a nun. The Abbeys were at Polsworth and Galloway, Scotland. Four centuries after her death, many miracles were reported at her tomb.

6. **Modwena of Killeavy,** Co. Down   c. 517
The two Modwenas have been confused since they shared the same feast day. However, they lived at quite different times. This one is more commonly called Edana and, according to the eminent Scottish historian, Skene, her name is the origin of the old name of Edinburgh, Dunedin. The historical connection of Edinburgh with Maiden Castle, refers to the convent

she established there in the fifth or sixth century (v. Cainnech 11 October).

7. **Maelruain of Tallaght** 792
Tallaght is regarded as the mother house of the Culdee movement which Maelruin co-founded with Aengus the Culdee (v. 11 March). This movement was intended to regularise the Rules of Irish monasticism, and to promote both the ascetic and the intellectual life. He collaborated with Aengus in producing the first catalogue of Irish Saints, the Martyrology of Tallaght.

8. **Killian, Colman, Tadhg** of Würzburg, Germany c. 689
(v. p. 42).

10. **Etto of Dompierre,** Belgium c. 670
An Abbot-Bishop who came to France with Fursa (v. p. 37). Up till recent times, his festival was held with such solemnity that an official mounted escort was provided for his relics. In 1920, Cardinal Mercier of Belgium sent a famous letter to the Irish Bishops at the time of the Irish Troubles, and named Etto as one of the Irish missionaries to whom Belgium was specially indebted.

11. **Drostan of Deer,** Scotland 6th century
A disciple of Columba who made him first Abbot of Deer Abbey near Buchan, Scotland. The Book of Deer, now in Cambridge University Library, is the oldest known work in Scottish Gaelic.

13. **John Travers, Chancellor of St. Patrick's Cathedral, Dublin**
(v. p. 92).

16. **Sinach MacDara of MacDara's Isle,** Connemara 6th century
This is the date on which fishermen traditionally converged on the island for an annual Mass. It is still a custom to dip sails or make the sign of the Cross in passing the island.

17. **Fredegand of Dorne,** Belgium 7th century
There has been a procession of the Blessed Sacrament in his honour on his feast day ever since his intercession is believed to have stopped a plague more than four centuries ago. He is widely venerated in North East France and Belgium.

18. **Minborinus of Cologne,** Germany 986
He led a group of Irish missionaries to Cologne where the Archbishop installed them with Minborinus as Abbot in the

Abbey of St. Martin's. At the same time, this was declared an Irish Abbey. Due to this influence, many churches in the diocese were dedicated to Irish Saints, including five churches and seven chapels to Brigid.

24. **Declan of Ardmore,** Co. Waterford   5th century
(v. Ch. 2).

29. **Kilian of Iniscaltra**   7th century
Kilian set up his monastery on the island of Iniscaltra. He is best known for his book on the Life of St. Brigid.

AUGUST

1. **Pellegrinus of Modena, Italy**   7th century
This name which simply means "pilgrim" is the only name known for this Irish Saint. Mount Pellegrino in the Italian Alps is named in his memory and was his hermitage. There is now a hospice, where services exist for travellers, including rescue facilities and free board for the needy.

5. **Abel of Rheims**   c. 750
Boniface, the English Apostle of Germany, had Abel appointed Archbishop of Rheims which was one of the most important Sees in the Church. French Kings at that time were crowned in Rheims. Abel was forced out by warring factions each determined to control the Archbishop. When he died, his tomb was elaborated to bear the cross of Archbishop and the fleur-de-lis of France.

9. **Nathy of Achonry**   c. 600
A powerful influence in Connaught, he founded his monastery in Achonry and was probably its first bishop.

10. **Blane of Kingarth, Isle of Bute,** Scotland   6th century
Of Irish nobility, he was born in Bute, and trained in Ireland. He was the nephew of St. Cathan (v. 11 May). He founded a famous monastery at Kingarth. His bell is preserved in the Cathedral of Dunblane which is named after him.

11. **Attracta of Achonry**   5th century
(v. p. 72).

12. **Molaise of Devenish,** Co. Fermanagh   564
Molaise is said to have brought from the Colosseum in Rome soil containing the blood of martyrs. His *cumdach* or book shrine containing manuscript Gospels is said to be the oldest in

Ireland. It is now in the National Museum in Dublin. He is one of the Twelve Apostles of Ireland (v. Finian, 12 December).

12. **Charles Mihan** (Martyred in England)   1639–1679
(v. p. 97).

13. **James Dowdall** (Martyred in England)   1598
(v. p. 92).

14. **Fachanan of Ross**   6th century
First Bishop of Ross and founder of Ross-Altair a noted centre of learning and pilgrimage. Patron of the Diocese of Ross.

19. **Cummian of Bobbio,** Italy   c. 730
King Liutprand of Lombardy erected the tomb of the Abbot Cummian and inscribed the monument with the pious wish that he might intercede for the response of his soul. Cummian's tomb is now under the new marble altar in this famous Irish Abbey, a national monument in Italy.

22. **Andrew of Fiesole,** Italy
The companion and Archdeacon of St. Donato of Fiesole (v. p. 48). He is much venerated in Tuscany and several churches are dedicated to him.

23. **Eoghan (Eugene) of Derry**   618
Patron of the Diocese of Derry. Said to have laboured in Britain and on the Continent as well as in Ireland.

25. **Michan of Dublin**   ???
The Church of St. Michan in Dublin became Protestant at the Reformation. Little is known of St. Michan, but the Church is famous for the incorruption of the bodies of Norman knights some of whom died as much as eight centuries ago. No satisfactory natural explanation has so far been given for this phenomenon.

26. **Gunifort of Pavia**   303
(v. p. 15).

28. **John Roche**   1588
(v. p. 94).

29. **Edmund Ignatius Rice**   1762–1844
(v. p. 99).

30. **Fiacre of Meaux,** France   c. 670
    (v. p. 38).

31. **Aidan of Lindisfarne**   651
    (v. p. 32).

SEPTEMBER

3. **Macanisius of Connor**   514
   Baptised by St. Patrick, he was the first Bishop of Connor, as
   well as Abbot of one of the larger communities of monks.

4. **Monessa**   456
   There are no details of her place of origin or her work. The
   reason is that according to a strong traditional belief she went
   straight to heaven after being baptised by St. Patrick.

7. **Ralph Corby** (Martyred in England)   1644
   (v. p. 97).

8. **Disibode of Disenberg,** Germany   c. 700
   His hermitage near Bingen was named Mount St. Disibode and
   later became the town of Disenberg. In the twelfth century,
   Hildegarde, the German "Sibyl of the Rhine" wrote a life of
   Disibode which she claimed had been revealed to her.

9. **Ciaran (Kieran) of Clonmacnoise**   512–545
   One of the Twelve Apostles of Ireland (v. Finian of Clonard
   12 December). It is said that he lived only seven months after
   founding the great School of Clonmacnoise, held by many to
   have been the most famous of all the Schools of Ireland. In
   1979, when Pope John Paul II came to Ireland, Clonmacnoise
   was the only School on his itinerary.

10. **Finian of Moville,** Co. Down   576
    There are many dedications to Finian in Scotland where he
    spent some twenty years. On his return, in 540, he founded
    Moville. The famous incident of the manuscript copied by St.
    Columba (v. Columba p. 25) concerns the Psalter of Finian.
    It is said that Finian was the first to bring into Irish scholar-
    ship the study of the Mosaic Law.

12. **Ailbhe of Emly,** Co. Tipperary   5th century
    (v. p. 16).

15. **Mirin of Paisley,** Scotland   6th century
    A contemporary of Columba, St. Mirin was a very powerful
    influence in the territory of Strathclyde, South of Glasgow. He

is honoured by both Catholics and Protestants. A unique testimony to this is the fact that he is the only Saint in Great Britain whose name has been adopted as patron of a famous football club, St. Mirren's of Paisley.

23. **Adamnan of Dull,** Scotland   624–704
It has been said by Montalembert, a noted French commentator on Irish monks, that the University of St. Andrews, the oldest Scottish University, developed from Adamnan's Abbey at Dull. Adamnan's Biography of Columba was the first complete biography of an Irish Saint and probably the beginning of Scottish literature. He was highly respected by the Anglo-Saxons and received very favourable mention in the writings of the Venerable Bede. He was elected ninth Abbot of Iona.

24. **Mansuy of Toul,** France   4th century
(v. p. 15).

24. **Grimonia of Soissons,** France   4th century
(v. p. 15).

25. **Finbar of Cork**   c. 623
His foundation by the river Lee was the beginning of Cork City of which he was the first Bishop. His island retreat at Gougane Barra, west of the city, is a place of pilgrimage on Gougane Sunday, the Sunday following his feast day. The Catholic island of Barra in the Scottish Hebrides is named after Finbar.

27. **Moengal of St. Gall,** Switzerland   c. 887
The cultural eminence of the great Swiss Abbey of St. Gall is generally believed to date from the time of Moengal. This was especially true of church music, a tradition founded by Moengal, in which the Abbey led all Christendom.

28. **Machan of Campsie,** Scotland   6th century
St. Machan went from Ireland to Campsie, north of Glasgow, where he is venerated as patron. There is an altar dedicated to him in the Cathedral in Glasgow.

OCTOBER

11. **Caimnech (Kenneth) of Killkenny**   527–600
He accompanied St. Columba on his visit to meet Brude, King of the Picts in Scotland, since Cainnech belonged to the Pictish race. He joined the Scottish Mission and is said to

have founded churches on the islands of Mull, Tiree, South Uist, Coll and Kintyre. He was the titular Saint of the Brethren of St. Kenneth who, until the Reformation, maintained the Abbey at Maiden Castle (v. Edana 6 July). He founded Abbeys at Aghaboe and Kilkenny which takes his name from him. The popularity of the name Kenneth in Scotland is a lasting tribute to the prestige of St. Cainnech, one of the Twelve Apostles of Ireland (v. Finian of Clonard, 12 December).

12. **Mobhi of Glasnevin, Dublin**   c. 544
His real name was Berchan, Mobhi being a term of affection. He is one of the Twelve Apostles of Ireland (v. Finian, 12 December). He had among his pupils, Columba of Iona, Comgall of Bangor, Ciaran of Clonmacnoise and Cainnech of Kilkenny. The unique feature of Mobhi's history is that, although he died of a plague about 545, his name is still normally quoted along with other eminent early saints, and this in spite of the fact that his monastery only lasted a few years.

13. **Colman of Melk,** Austria   1012
(v. p. 43).

16. **Gall of St. Gall,** Switzerland   540–630
(v. p. 46).

16. **Eliph of Toul,** France   c. 362
(v. p. 15).

21. **Wendel of Tholey,** Germany   6th century
(v. p. 73).

21. **Fintan Munnu of Taghmon,** Co. Wexford   635
Arrived in Iona in 597, just after the death of St. Columba, to be told that Columba had left instructions that he was not to be enrolled as his destiny was to found his own Abbey. This he did at Taghmon. He is said to have been afflicted with leprosy and to have prayed to be so afflicted as it added to his spiritual merit.

22. **Donato of Fiesole,** Italy   876
(v. p. 48).

24. **Tadhg MacCarthy of Cork**   1455–1492
(v. p. 91).

26. **Albuin (Wittan) of Fritzlar,** Germany   c. 760
Another of the Irish monks who worked with St. Boniface, the

English Apostle of Germany. Boniface made Albuin Bishop of Fritzlar where he is venerated under the German name of Wittan.

27. **Oran of Oransay,** Scotland   548
Some historians claim that Oran was in Iona before St. Columba. This is based on the fact that the ancient cemetery there was called Reilig Oran.

29. **Colman of Kilmacduagh,** Co. Clare   c. 632
A recluse, he lived in seclusion in the Burren in Co. Clare. The tradition is that angels brought King Guaire to him by the simple method of removing an entire feast from his table before his eyes. The King gave chase and was led to Colman who was undergoing a Lenten fast. The "road of the dishes" is the legendary name for this journey. Between them, the King and Colman founded the monastery at Kilmacduagh (Church of the Son of Duas, i.e. Colman). Colman became the first bishop. The "Leaning tower of Kilmacduagh", 112 feet high is almost twice as old as the famous Tower of Pisa.

31. **Foillan of Fosses,** Belgium   655
The March of Foillan is a spectacular procession every seven years in September in honour of this Irish saint at Fosses. His relics have an official mounted guard and salutes are fired at seven different stages of the route. Foillan was a brother of St. Fursa of Peronne (v. p. 37) who left him as Abbot of Burghcastle in Suffolk when he went over to France. Foilan also went to France after Fursey's death and was eventually martyred near Nivelles. He is widely venerated in Northern France.

31. **Bee of St. Bees,** Cumberland   7th century
An Irish princess, said to have fled on the eve of her wedding to consecrate her life to God. She received her vows from Aidan of Lindisfarne (v. p. 33). She set up her convent on the promontory now named St. Bees. There is a medieval legend that statements sworn on her bracelet were accepted without further question.

NOVEMBER

2. **Erc of Slane**   c. 512
It was Erc who, during St. Patrick's confrontation with the druids in the Hill of Slane, was the only one to do him homage.

Later St. Patrick ordained him priest and bishop. At his church in Tralee, he trained Brendan the Navigator (v. p. 49) from the age of six till he was ordained. His most famous establishment was his School at Slane where the Merovingian King Dagobert II was said to have been a student.

4. **Malachy of Armagh**   1094–1148
(v. p. 94).

6. **ALL THE SAINTS OF IRELAND**

7. **Florence of Strasbourg**   687
Bishop of Strasbourg, where he built St. Thomas' Abbey for Irish monks. He is buried in the Church of St. Thomas.

7. **Patrick Fleming**   1599–1631
(v. p. 94).

9. **Benen (Benignus) of Armagh**   467
Benen was only a child when he became a disciple of St. Patrick, and never left him. One of the most famous legends of Ireland tells of the occasion when St. Patrick with his eight companions and the boy Benen were going to Tara to confront the High King, they were miraculously changed into deer and so avoided the attempts of the King's guards to intercept them. The fawn in the rear, according to the legend, was Benen. He succeeded St. Patrick as the second Bishop of Armagh.

10. **John of Ratzeburg,** Germany   c. 1066
Came to Germany with St. Marianus of Ratisbon (v. p. 45). He was made Bishop of Ratzeburg and was martyred in East Germany in 1066.

10. **Catherine McAuley**   1778–1841
(v. p. 98).

11. **Bertuin of Namur,** Belgium   698
Founded a church and School at Maloigne, near Namur. He was trained in a monastery in England and consecrated there as bishop.

12. **Livinius of Ghent**   c. 650
Left Ireland as a bishop with several companions. The whole group were martyred at Ghent in Belgium where his relics are enshrined and venerated.

12. **Machar (Mochumma) of Aberdeen**   6th century
Said to have been the first Bishop of Aberdeen. The water from his well was at one time used for baptisms in Aberdeen Cathedral.

12. **Sinell of Cleenish,** Co. Fermanagh   6th century
He is one of the Twelve Apostles of Ireland (v. Finian of Clonard 12 December). He set up his monastery on Cleenish Island in Lough Erne, Co. Fermanagh. It was regarded as one of the most rigorous in Ireland. His most illustrious student was Columbanus of Luxeuil (v. p. 35).

13. **Caillin of Ferns**   7th century
Associated with Aiden of Ferns (v. 31 January). He is best known for an ancient tradition according to which he turned a group of druids into stone.

13. **Kilian of Aubigny,** France   7th century
A kinsman of Fiacre of Meaux (v. p. 38), he joined him in his mission and soon set up his own Abbey at Aubigny near Arras. His body is enshrined in his own Church in Aubigny where he is the object of great veneration. He is the only Irishman said to have been offered the Papacy, which he declined to accept.

14. **Laurence O'Toole, Archbishop of Dublin**   1123–1180
(v. p. 61).

15. **Fintan of Rheinau,** Germany   878
He was captured by Viking pirates but escaped from the Orkneys. Two years later, he made a pilgrimage to Rome after which he settled on the island of Rheinau, near Schaffhausen on the Rhine. He is said to have heard angels talking to him in the Gaelic tongue. His Calendar is preserved in the library of the University of Zurich, Switzerland, and his Missal is in the library of St. Gall, Switzerland.

18. **Mombolus of Lagny,** France   7th century
He was one of the monks at Lagny and became Abbot but was compelled to resign because of the severity of his Rule. He retired to a life of total seclusion. His cult is very strong in the Diocese of Meaux, and his body was enshrined with great ceremony two centuries after his death by the Bishops of Cambrai and Noyon.

23. **Columbanus of Luxeuil,** France   543–615
(v. p. 35).

24. **Colman of Cloyne** 530–606

MacLenini, the royal bard of Munster, became a Christian when he rescued from a lake the stolen shrine of St. Ailbhe. Brenden of Clonfert (v. p. 49) baptised him and named him Colman. In due course, he became the first Bishop of Cloyne.

27. **Fergus the Pict** 8th century

A powerful influence in the area between Aberdeen and Wick on the north coast of Scotland. There is a town called St. Fergus near Buchan and other dedications. He is buried at Glamis, a central location of Shakespeare's famous Scottish tragedy, *Macbeth*. Fergus was much venerated by Scottish kings. He was the Scottish representative at the Council of Rome in 721. Reformers made strong efforts to destroy his cult which is currently growing, especially in the Paisley area of Renfrewshire where a new Church has been dedicated to him and the nearby town of Ferguslie is said to be named after him.

27. **Virgilus (Fearghal) of Saltzburg** 784
(v. p. 65).

29. **Brendan of Birr,** Co. Offaly 573

He is one of the Twelve Apostles of Ireland (v. Finian of Clonard 12 December). Often confused with his famous namesake Brendan of Clonfert (v. p. 49). A popular legend has it that Columba of Iona had a vision of Brendan of Birr's death and said a Requiem Mass for him many days in advance of confirmation of the death. According to another tradition, it was he and not the other Brendan who was chosen by lot among the Twelve Apostles of Ireland to go in search of the Land of Promise, but he was prevented by his health.

DECEMBER

3. **Eloquius of Lagny,** France c. 665

He was one of the companions of Fursa of Peronne (v. p. 37) whom he succeeded as Abbot of Langny where he was buried. He was later interred in the Irish Abbey of Waulsort, Belgium.

7. **Buite of Monasterboice,** Co. Louth c. 521

The most famous legend concerning Buite relates how he restored to life the son of Nectan, King of the Scottish Picts. In return, the King installed Buite in Kirkbuddo, the Church of Buite. About the year 500, he founded his Irish School at

Monasterboice which became celebrated when the Viking raids threatened to put an end to the cultural output of the great Schools. Buite's School became the centre of Irish sculpture and the Crosses of Monasterboice are now world-famous.

11. **The Two Emers** 5th century
These were the daughters of Miluic who were given the veil by St. Patrick and installed in what is said to have been the first convent in Ireland (v. Guasacht 24 January).

12. **Finian of Clonard** c. 549
He founded Clonard about 520 and is regarded, like Enda of Aran (v. 21 March) as a father of Irish monasticism. His monastery somehow survived the Viking era and other disasters until it was suppressed at the Reformation. Finian trained so many great Irish saints that it became the custom to speak of the Twelve Apostles of Ireland, from among his students.

13. **Colm of Terryglass** 549
He is one of the Twelve Apostles of Ireland (v. Finian of Clonard 12 December). His most famous foundation was Terryglass on the Shannon where he died of the plague in 549. He also founded Clonenagh, along with St. Fintan, its most famous Abbot (v. 17 February) and Iniscultra.

14. **Fingar and Piala** 5th century
A long-standing tradition has it that these two, son and daughter of an Irish King, were martyred at Hayle, Cornwall along with other companions.

18. **Flannan of Killaloe** 7th century
First Bishop of Killaloe. He also laboured in the Hebrides and gave his name to the Flannan Isles.

19. **Samthann of Clonbroney,** Co. Longford 739
A nun whose cult was made famous when St. Virgilius (Fearghal) of Salzburg (v. p. 65) introduced it on the Continent.

19. **Macarius of Würzburg** 1153
Due to the prominence of the cult of Kilian and his companions in Würzburg (v. p. 42), this city became a centre for Irish pilgrims and the Irish Abbey at Ratisbon sent Macarius to open an Irish Abbey at Würzburg. As a result, this city has long had the reputation of being a centre of Irish antiquities.

Macarius is very much venerated there and, in 1818, his remains were enshrined in the Marienkapelle in Würzburg.

24. **Mochua of Timahoe,** Co. Kildare   c. 657
Venerated both at Timahoe (Teach Mochua – The House of Mochua) and at Derenish, Co. Cavan which he founded and where he is buried.

26. **Tathai of Llandathan,** Wales   6th century
Probably the most famous of Irish saints in Wales. His School at Llandathan, named after him, was one of the most noted in Wales. Its most famous student was the great Celtic scholar, Cadoc.

28. **Maughold of the Isle of Man**   488
Said to have been a pirate converted by St. Patrick who sent him to the Isle of Man to expiate his sins. Traditionally, he is honoured as the Apostle of the Isle of Man.

Epilogue

At the conclusion of such a work as this, many questions seem to be left unanswered. It could be said that this impression is shared by the author, when so much material is confined within the space of a small volume. This calls for a treatment which, of necessity, confines the facts to the bare minimum. In that process, essential basic elements are highlighted to a greater extent than they would be in a wider context. They are also referred to with the briefest of explanations.

Readers are likely to include many who in their formative years have heard a great deal about the Irish saints. Too often, they comment that the total picture is one of sanctity of a high order, and that one saint is a replica of another. They are, many would say, stereotypes. The human side is too often left out in presenting the lives of individual saints.

The accounts of personalities described here have stressed the individuality of each of them. They were all people in their own right. Indeed, it could be said that those among them who have emerged in the public image as the most eminent figures, have been precisely those whose individual personalities were most marked. Equally these were the saints who left the deepest impression on the society within which they laboured.

Columba of Iona, for example, saw his mission as essentially one of civilising a restless people. He conceived it as his task to spread the Gospel of Christianity which he combined with the best elements of his native culture. As a result, he laid the foundations of an entire nation. St. Fiacre of Meaux has lived on in the memory of his devotees as one who offered his services to suffering humanity. The devotion to St. Dymphna is expressed principally by compassion for the mentally afflicted.

So far as possible then, the contribution to society has been stressed in all cases. In a longer book, it would have been interesting to deal in greater depth with the lessons to be learned from the Rules under which the Irish monks chose to live, for these reflected strongly a conscious reaction against excesses in the society in which they lived. So their fasting, often described as excessive, showed their concern to correct the material excesses they saw in the leaders of society. In the same way, they obviously excluded alcohol from their establishments, while their constant demands for sexual morality seem to have been dictated by immoral behaviour outside the monastery.

On reflection, it can hardly be said that the Irish monks withdrew from society and lived a life of isolation. Clearly, they went out and provided mankind with specific fields to develop. To say that they were a stereotyped group, offering only sanctity, is not consistent with the facts. Fiacre is one of the first on record who was prepared to try to cure syphilitics. Until Dymphna founded the tradition, society was not prepared to recognise a need to care for the mentally sick. The clear and early aversion of Irish monks to the abuse of alcohol was centuries in advance of what is now regarded as a social requirement.

Reference to the rules drawn up for Irish monks in various establishments leads one to speculate on a point which has exercised the minds of more than one scholar. This is the curious fact that, although Irish monks enjoyed such eminence, even pre-eminence, for so long, no Irish Rule survived to perpetuate this in the form of an ancient and continuing order. Instead, the Benedictines, and others later, were to absorb ancient Irish abbeys under their Rule, and the Irish origins of the establishments became largely an interesting fact of history.

One of the reasons for this was that monastic Rules tended, in the early Irish tradition, to be established by each founder and there was no one Rule which prevailed. To be sure, the Rule of Iona was widespread in Scotland and in the Columban establishments in Ireland. In retrospect, it was perhaps unfortunate that the possibility of a great Irish Order comparable to the Benedictines, arising out of this, was offset by the confusion caused by the so-called Irish practices, particularly strong in the traditions of St. Columba.

It so happened in the early centuries that the Holy See was preoccupied with problems of orthodoxy, and of ensuring that liturgical practices were uniform throughout the Church. The so-called Celtic Church, which it might be added included Ireland and the Celts of Britain, was at variance with the official view on a number of issues. The one most commonly quoted was the date of Easter, fixed by Rome on one system and by the Celtic Church on a different one. Another issue was the tonsure, on which

Irish monks had their own ideas. Again, they were less orthodox in their administration of certain Sacraments, especially baptism.

These are not issues which could be considered as doctrinal. In the early days of the Church, they had a special importance at a time when Rome was establishing its authority. So it may well have appeared to the Holy See that Irish abbeys, governed by Rules which reflected Irish traditions, should pass under the control of Orders which followed Rome in all respects.

Clearly, such issues as have been discussed above are far beyond the scope of such a book as this. They had, however, to be referred to at various points since they played a great part in the lives of personalities described. Irish people have often been confused by the comments they read on the Celtic Church. It has even been remarked that no Irishman has ever been Pope. The ancient tradition, created by the early Irish monks of opposition to orthodoxy, as it was defined at the time, may have been part of the reason.

These and other issues could and would be part of a wider survey of the whole topic of Irish sanctity. As it is, the book is an attempt to bring together the salient features of the whole story. Those who seek further information will find a vast body of literature of Irish and non-Irish origin, which has made of Irish sanctity in all its aspects, the basis of a major field of study. If this book succeeds in creating the interest to pursue the matter further, its main purpose is achieved and, indeed, the effort of writing it will be justified.

Bibliography

Bander, Peter, *The Prophecies of St. Malachy and St. Columb-kille.* Gerrards Cross, England, Colin Smythe, 4th ed. 1979.

Bede, The Venerable, *Ecclesiastical History of England.* Edited by Bertram Colgrave and R. A. B. Mynors, Oxford, Clarendon Press, 1969.

Bieler, Ludwig, *Works of St. Patrick.* Westminster, Maryland, U.S.A., Newman Press, 1953.

Butler, Aidan, *Lives of the Saints.* Edited by Herbert Thurston and Donald Attwater, New York, J. P. Kennedy and Sons, 1953.

Catholic Encyclopedia, New. Washington, D.C., Catholic University of America, 1967.

Carty, Francis, *Two and Fifty Irish Saints.* Dublin, James Duffy and Company Ltd., 1941.

Carty, Francis, *Irish Saints in Ten Countries.* Dublin, James Duffy and Company Ltd., 1942.

Curtayne, Alice, *St. Brigid of Ireland.* London, Methuen and Company, Ltd., 1942.

Curtis, Edmund, *History of Ireland.* London, Methuen and Company, Ltd., 1942.

Daniel-Rops, H., *The Miracle of Ireland.* Translated by The Earl of Wicklow, Baltimore U.S.A.

D'Arcy, Mary Ryan, *The Saints of Ireland.* St. Paul, U.S.A., Irish-American Cultural Institute, 1974.

Donaldson, Gordon and Morpeth, Robert S., *Dictionary of Scottish History.* Edinburgh, John Donald, Publishers, 1977.

Encyclopaedia Britannica. Chicago, William Benton, Publisher, 1971.

Farmer, David Hugh, *The Oxford Dictionary of Saints.* Oxford, Clarendon Press, 1978.

Forristal, Desmond, *Oliver Plunkett.* Dublin, Veritas Publications, 1975.

Glynn, Sir Joseph, *The Life of Matt Talbot.* Dublin, the Catholic Truth Society, 1925.

Gougaud, Dom Louis, *Gaelic Pioneers of Christianity*. Translated by Victor Collins, Dublin, M. H. Gill & Son, Ltd., 1923.

Henry, Françoise, *Irish Art in the Early Christian Period*. Ithaca, New York, Cornell University Press, 1965.

Kenney, J. F., *Sources for Early History of Ireland*. Vol. 1, Ecclesiastical, New York, Columbia University Press, 1929.

Letts, Winifred M. *St. Patrick the Travelling Man*. London, Ivor Nicholson and Watson, Ltd., 1932.

Little, George A., *Brendan the Navigator*. Dublin, M. H. Gill and Son, Ltd., 1923.

Logan, Patrick, *The Holy Wells of Ireland*. Gerrards Cross, England, Colin Smythe, 1980.

McNeill, Eoin, *St Patrick*. Dublin, Clonmore and Reynolds, Ltd., 1964.

McNeill, Eoin, *Phases of Irish History*. Dublin, M. H. Gill and Son, Ltd., 1937.

McNeill, John Thomas, *The Celtic Churches*. Chicago, Chicago University Press, 1974.

Moran, Cardinal, *Irish Saints in Great Britain*. Dublin, Brown and Nolan, 1879.

Mould, D. C. Pochin, *Scotland of the Saints*. London, Batsford, 1952.

Mould, D. C. Pochin, *Ireland of the Saints*. London, Batsford, 1953.

Neeson, Eoin, *Book of Irish Saints*. Cork, Mercier Press, 1967.

O'Fiaich, Cardinal Tomas, *Oliver Plunkett – Ireland's New Saint*. Dublin, Veritas Publications, 1975.

Ryan, John, *Irish Monasticism*. Dublin, Talbot Press, Ltd., 1931.

Severin, Tim, *The Brendan Voyage*. London, Hutchinson, 1978.

Simpson, W. George, *The Celtic Church in Scotland*. Aberdeen, University Studies, III, 1934.

Skene, W. F., *Celtic Scotland*, 3 volumes, Edinburgh.

Tommasini, Fra Anselmo, *Irish Saints in Italy*. London, Sands and Company, Ltd., 1937.